P9-BZA-070

He was standing with his head pressed against the wall and

CRYING.

I CAME UP AND PUT MY HANDS ON HIM . . .

"I love you so," he said, "you and Dad. I want to live happily with you."

"Tony dear, we love you so much too. And as long as we remember that, nothing else is really important. Things will turn out fine. You'll see."

He raised his head, his marvelous eyes, so trusting, so clear.

"Will they, Ma? You really believe they will?"

"I know it, Tony. . . ."

I got out. I fled across the hall into my own room and locked the door. For a long time I sat there in the dark, trembling before something terrible and unknown.

"Intensely moving . . . An extraordinary book written with simplicity and humility."
Book World

Other SIGNET Titles You Will Enjoy

☐ **LISTEN TO THE SILENCE by David W. Elliott.** A total and unique experience—gripping, poignant, most often, shattering. A fourteen-year-old boy narrates the chronicle of events that lead him into, through, and out of an insane asylum. "Each page has the ring of unmistakable truth . . . a well-written, tour de force, another **Snake Pit** . . ." —The New York Times Book Review.

(#Q4513—95¢)

☐ **I NEVER PROMISED YOU A ROSE GARDEN by Hannah Green.** A beautifully written novel of rare insight about a young girl's courageous fight to regain her sanity in a mental hospital.

(#Q3853—95¢)

☐ **THE AUTOBIOGRAPHY OF A SCHIZOPHRENIC GIRL by Marguerite Sechehaye.** The classic case history of a young girl who retreats completely into a world of fantasy, and her slow recovery.

(#T4117—75¢)

☐ **LISA, BRIGHT AND DARK by John Neufeld.** Lisa is slowly going mad but her symptoms—even an attempted suicide—fail to alert her parents or teachers to her illness. She finds compassion only from three girlfriends who band together to provide what they call "group therapy."

(#P4387—60¢)

☐ **THE STORY OF SANDY by Susan Stanhope Wexler.** The moving true story of a foster parent's courageous fight for the sanity of a deeply disturbed little boy.

(#Q4517—95¢)

THE NEW AMERICAN LIBRARY, INC.,
P.O. Box 999, Bergenfield, New Jersey 07621

Please send me the SIGNET BOOKS I have checked above. I am enclosing $_____(check or money order—no currency or C.O.D.'s). Please include the list price plus 15¢ a copy to cover mailing costs.

Name_____

Address_____

City_____State_____Zip Code_____
Allow at least 3 weeks for delivery

This Stranger, My Son

A MOTHER'S STORY

by Louise Wilson

A SIGNET BOOK from
NEW AMERICAN LIBRARY
TIMES MIRROR

COPYRIGHT © 1968 BY LOUISE WILSON

All rights reserved. This book or parts thereof must not be reproduced in any form without permission. For information address G. P. Putnam's Sons, 200 Madison Ave., New York, New York 10016.

All names in this book have been changed. Any resemblance to any living person is coincidental.

Library of Congress Catalog Card Number: 68-12105

This is an authorized reprint of a hardcover edition published by G. P. Putnam's Sons. Published simultaneously in the Dominion of Canada by Longmans Canada Limited, Toronto.

SEVENTH PRINTING

SIGNET TRADEMARK REG. U.S. PAT. OFF. AND FOREIGN COUNTRIES
REGISTERED TRADEMARK—MARCA REGISTRADA
HECHO EN CHICAGO, U.S.A.

SIGNET, SIGNET CLASSICS, SIGNETTE, MENTOR AND PLUME BOOKS *are published by The New American Library, Inc., 1301 Avenue of the Americas, New York, New York 10019*

FIRST PRINTING, JANUARY, 1969

PRINTED IN THE UNITED STATES OF AMERICA

This Stranger,
My Son

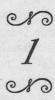

1

WE left the taxi at the gate and walked in. The wall split the summer afternoon in two; outside a gritty urban wilderness of elevated tracks, used-car lots and shabby row houses; inside, old copper beeches drawing shady circles on a vivid lawn and a young girl in a pink dress reading on a bench. At the top of the drive was the main building. Its fine Georgian portico might have belonged to a library in a suburban town or to the admissions office of a New England college. But here, behind the pointed stone and ivy-covered wings, if you knew where to look up, at the top you could discern the windows with the ornamental ironwork discreetly and firmly barred.

In the airy lobby we took our usual places near the door with the polished placard: Dr. Howard Brewster. There were magazines on a table, but neither Jack nor I had the patience to read. Nor did we speak to one another. We had our own thoughts. Strangely enough, I do not think that either of us was very much afraid. By now we knew what we had to bear; each of us knew that the other would do his best and that best would be good enough.

Still, ordinary occurrences take on unnatural significance when you are waiting for something, some great shaping or concluding event in your life. A ringing telephone was startling; the muffled rubber-heeled tread of a passing nurse ominous. A boy came uncertainly into the lobby. It was painful to look at him, but there was no place else to look except down at my shoes. He was about nineteen, like Tony, and lanky like him. Like him too, he stood there, a living question, an agony of indecision in the center of the enormous room. After a long time he was able to make up his mind and walked slowly outside and down the steps.

I wondered what we would do if our son were to come out and find us here. But surely they would have made certain that Tony would not be in this part of the building now.

The door opened. "Doctor Brewster will see you," the secretary said.

These rooms, these inner sanctums, all resemble one another, and their calculated cheer is saddening to me. The inevitable sunny prints, Van Gogh's Provençal fields; the tended, flourishing philodendron in ceramic pots. All these things which speak with such encouragement of green life and health. All these things which tell of hope and the good things of the world, the good simple things that lie beyond the reach of those who, after God alone knows what awful struggle, have at last been brought here.

"Well," said Dr. Brewster, rising from behind

his desk, "right on time, aren't you? You must have started before dawn." He had the easy manner of many large, ruddy men, a reassuring manner for a psychiatrist or for anyone who has to deal with the very ill.

But Jack was beyond reassurance that day. "We came last night and then stayed in a hotel," he said quickly, "so as to be on time. How has Tony been this last week?"

"I should say that he's somewhat more relaxed. I had a nice talk with him yesterday. Of course, he wants desperately to get out of here."

We waited. I felt the sweat in my palms. Was this man, perhaps, at long last, the final answer? No, not really. I knew better than that. But at least he might give us an immediate solution, an answer to: What do we do right now?

And on his desk I saw the pile of papers, a typewritten sheaf as thick as a dictionary, the long and bitter history of Tony, our son. There they lay, all the detailed, heaped-up records, the questionnaire that Jack and I had answered for the doctors, the transcripts and reports from the school psychologists and now from the various personnel of this hospital, from social workers and psychiatrists; all the painful searching, the interviews, the harried years, all there in black on white. A life on paper.

"We've finished with our study of Tony," Dr. Brewster said now. "I think we know all we have to know." He began to speak rapidly and earnestly. "I'm sure it will relieve you to learn that Tony will not require further hospitalization. We're turning him out into the world to live." He smiled and waited, so it seemed, for our reaction of joy.

But Jack was always cautious and skeptical. "Doctor," he said, "I'm a surgeon. In your field as much a layman as though I were not a physician at all. What do you mean by 'live'? Live how? And how sick, exactly, is Tony? I admit at this point to absolute confusion."

"Tony is very sick; you know that, of course. But he does, fortunately, have enough reserve control so that he can, to some extent, function in ordinary life. For the present, he ought to be given his chance to do so. Naturally, one cannot say that he will never have to be hospitalized. Only for the present, happily, he doesn't."

No hospital! My relief could have exploded equally well into tears or laughter. No pottery or basket weaving or other gloomy occupational therapy; no long, gray, death-in-life! Reprieve now, for who knew how long. . . .

My husband forged straight ahead, earnestly. "You must remember, Doctor Brewster, how many conflicting reports there were when we brought Tony here for study. We have never really had a diagnosis, and—"

"Schizophrenia, if you want to label it. The boy is a paranoid schizophrenic."

Suddenly the world went still. *Schizophrenia, if you want a label.* Tony's dark blue eyes, his beautiful, rare smile. And the ugly contortions of his rage. Most of all, his fear. Terror and fear.

"It's a word, that's all, a word that covers a large, loose category." Dr. Brewster leaned back in the tilting chair and looked away at a point on the wall behind us. "It's like saying 'tree.' There are all kinds, firs, elms, pines. So there are many kinds and degrees of schizophrenia. The paranoid, like Tony, is distinguished by certain factors such as suspicion of others, the conviction that 'people are against him.' He also has feelings of grandiosity; he thinks himself better than other people, more powerful, able to do anything he wants to do. But we've talked over all these traits often enough. There's nothing I can tell you about the way Tony behaves that you don't already know."

"I suppose not, except," Jack said, "the course of the sickness, how much better or worse it can get. Of course, I know you can't make any promises. I thought only that, statistically, there might be some indication . . ."

Dr. Brewster shook his head. "There is so much shifting about on the part of any one patient that it defies prognosis. He can be having hallucinations one week, perhaps even require restraint. And then he might be back on a responsible job a month or so later. Or the other way around. It can be a very fluid condition, you must bear that in mind. Or it can be a permanent, incapacitating crippler."

"Then what are we to do?"

The reply was sure. "Keep him busy, above all. No idle time, no days without purpose. Since Tony is intellectually superior, he definitely ought to go on to college."

"His College Boards were all in the seven hundreds," I ventured timidly.

Dr. Brewster nodded. "So he certainly ought to have a try at it. The only problem is where to live.

That's the question. He couldn't survive in a dormitory."

"No," Jack said, "he wouldn't last a week. He'd be a marked man, living closely with a crowd of boys."

There was a long silence. "Perhaps a furnished room," Dr. Brewster suggested. "He could live in this area, go to classes and continue here as an outpatient, seeing me."

"He wouldn't see you," I said quickly. "Tony won't go to a psychiatrist unless he's forced to. So he'd be all alone in a room. Nobody would talk to him since he doesn't talk to anyone. How long could he bear it, do you think?"

"One can only try," Dr. Brewster replied.

"Is there a possibility of ever coming home?" Jack asked, hesitating.

At the thought of Tony's coming home, a sharp fear rose in me. All that to go through again. I realized I was relieved to hear Dr. Brewster deny the possibility.

"I'm afraid you'll have to accept the fact that Tony will not be coming home for a long time," he said. "The situation wasn't tenable when he lived at home and he is no different now. With a person as hostile as Tony family life presents too many involvements." He turned to me. "How many other children did you say you have?"

"Three. Jane is seventeen, two years younger than Tony, and we have fifteen-year-old twins, Freddy and Sarah. They're all well, healthy and happy." I was talking too much, but it was something I could not resist. I was counting my riches.

"Good. And you owe them something. Particularly in their own vulnerable adolescence, you owe them a peaceful house to which they can bring their friends without being embarrassed by this odd and different brother. No, there can be no doubt. Tony is not to come home."

"What if he should do so anyway?" Jack asked. "You know he keeps saying we have no right to keep him out of his home. He told my wife last week on the telephone that—God pity him—he was going to get a lawyer to force us to take him back in."

"Well, of course, that's just nonsense."

"I know. But suppose he should appear at the door and refuse to leave?"

"Then you will have to remove him forcibly."

Call my thoughts snobbish or mean, but I had a sudden feeling that such public violence took place in families where drunken husbands beat their wives. This just didn't happen to people like us.

"But surely," Jack went on, "Tony isn't unique? You must have seen so many patients who are in this half-way state, not well enough to live in normal situations yet not sick enough for a hospital. What do they do?"

"Of course there are others, thousands of them. In any skid-row section of a large city, you'd be surprised how many of those derelicts are victims of schizophrenia. You've heard stories, I'm sure, about educated men who have given up, just dropped out of life. They're a kind of floater population. Strangers, on the fringe of life, just strong enough to hold together."

"What happens to them?" I said hesitantly.

"Some of them go on like that to the end. Some grow worse and eventually have to be hospitalized. Some, when the going gets too hard, commit suicide."

Well, I thought, *you asked for it.*

"I'm afraid to put Tony into a room here by himself," I said.

"I can understand that."

"If only there were someone who would give him a home. On a farm, perhaps, where he could work and still be watched over. We'd pay anything, gladly."

There was no answer. I tried again.

"In all this country—and you say there are thousands of people like Tony—in all this country, there is no place?"

"Unfortunately, none."

"None," I repeated dully.

Jack thought I had asked a question. "Louise, the doctor has told us there is no place."

"I'm sorry."

Dr. Brewster stood up, just as his secretary opened the door. The interview was over.

"I always tell parents in your position," he concluded kindly, "that they must abandon the normally excellent habit of making plans. For patients of this sort you simply cannot make plans. If I were in your place I would just take each day as it comes. I would get up every morning and pray for strength to get through that one day."

We shook hands. "Tony can remain here in the open ward while you look around. You can be thinking about some classes in this city and a room for him in the neighborhood. Or any other arrangement that comes to mind. Then let me hear from you."

We were out in the June light again, walking toward the gate. We did not speak. For even though you are with each other and even though you love each other, on a day like this you are in a strange way alone and lonely in your helpless fear. It comes upon you like a blow, this realization of your helplessness. You who have always been able to cope with things quite sensibly and strongly, suddenly can now do nothing. And yet it is really not so sudden; it is rather a final recognition of something that has been there, hidden from yourself and denied for a long, long time. It has been with you so long and still, even now, you can hardly conceive of it or that this is you and this is happening to you.

2

HOW did it begin? The past is obscure. At what instant in time does one fall in love? At what single moment does a man begin to die or did we begin to "lose" Tony?

I cannot tell, so I shall begin in the beginning.

He was a wanted child. Jack and I had been married for three years. He had finished a residency in surgery and entered the Navy just when the Second World War broke out. I had a job in the social-work department of a New York hospital and could be on hand whenever he returned on leave. When I became pregnant he wanted me to return to my parents in Ohio. He wanted to know that the child and I would be cared for while he was overseas.

So not too unhappily I went back to the shabby Victorian house in which I had grown up. I had solid faith that Jack would survive the war. I don't know how I came to have it but happily it was given to me to have that faith. I knew that the war would be won and that life would begin again for all of us.

The doctor who had brought me into the world was too old for the service but not too old to deliver my child. He did so with deft and easy skill. I remember the tender, damp spring night, the kind voice saying, "Well, Louise, here's your son." There was a feeling of immense comfort and a soft surge of sleep. Vaguely I knew when my father and mother came into my room. It must have been another room, some hours later, and they said something about a cablegram, theirs to Jack or his to us. And Dad said Tony was a handsome boy ... He *was* a handsome boy. Not one of our three subsequent children could compare with him. Even in infancy his bones had a sculpted beauty. You could see that his face would be long, that he would have a long, straight nose, a graceful mouth.

We put him to sleep that spring in the carriage under the maple by the kitchen door. Dad looked down at him one day, and said, "I hope life will be good to him."

Quite recently I came across his baby book. There is a list of gifts, all the hand-knitted bonnets, the silver drinking cup with "Anthony" engraved upon it, the blue and red carriage robe sent by Jack from England. And the letters to me from Jack along with the letters to Tony from Jack: "To be opened when you are fifteen," "When you are twenty-one," "When you are married." There they are, written because no man could be certain then that he would ever come home and he had wanted to leave something of himself to his son in the event that he did not. There they lie unopened. Perhaps Jack has forgotten that he ever wrote them.

The first months of Tony's life passed quietly. I wrote to Jack every day and waited for his letters; weeks went by without mail from him and then half a dozen letters arrived together. Once a week I went downtown to the movies with my friends Nora and Julie, whose husbands were also overseas. I hemmed kitchen towels, bought home magazines and drew up color schemes for the house Jack, Tony and I would live in someday. I had always had a small talent for painting and I returned to art classes twice a week. It gave me a good feeling of accomplishment. In the brutal heat of a Midwestern afternoon I would carry Tony downstairs to catch a faint breeze on the porch, bathe him with cool cloths and sing to him as I did my painting.

He did not sleep well. Noise bothered him; the distant backfiring of an automobile or the creaking of Dad's step on the stairs woke him into startled crying. Or sometimes for no reason at all he lay awake and wailed. Mother said that he had gas and she used to pick him up and walk with him, up and down the long front porch, patting and thumping between the shoulder blades. As long as she walked he did not cry. As soon as he was laid down the crying resumed in a kind of breathless, weeping protest.

There was nothing physically wrong with him. He did not have colic. He gained weight steadily, cut his teeth and sat up on schedule. Our doctor gave me his opinion.

"You have a fine baby here, but I think you've spoiled him. Babies learn quickly, you know, and he has already found out that all he has to do is cry and you'll pick him up. Just try letting him cry it out a few nights and he'll learn."

So I let him cry, and he cried all night, long choking sobs that were agony to hear. Around six in the morning he fell asleep but woke again at eight. For four nights the process was repeated. Then I could stand it no longer. I picked him up and held him until the comfort he seemed to feel from being held brought sleep.

I went to another doctor, a young pediatrician who had just completed his training. "Tony is a hyperkinetic baby," he told me. Unlike the old family doctor, he at least believed me when I told him how little Tony slept.

"You will just have to live with this until he gets over it."

In time and to a certain extent he did, although he has always suffered from a degree of insomnia. Whether this early sleeplessness "meant anything," I do not know. I only set it down because that's the way it happened.

But then such relatively small troubles were forgotten: Jack was coming home. He brought with him a splendid offer from a surgeon who needed an associate. The town was not far from Jack's old family home in New England where his brother Russell still lived. This was just what we had dreamed about: a country life which could somehow be combined with Jack's career; perhaps even an old farmhouse to remodel.

"Sort of having one's cake and eating it too," Jack said.

Everything moved in a daze of speed. It was just three months from his return to the gilded fall day when at last we turned the key in the lock of our own house.

It was an old saltbox with great fireplaces and tiny windows, seven miles from the town where Jack was to work. We had been very frugal during the war years and now we had funds enough to set the house in proper order. We painted it barn red; we refurbished the rail fence around the front yard and repaired the barn which was to house the ponies we hoped to buy for all the children we hoped to have.

Russell and his wife Ann had driven over to stay for a few days and help us settle in. By the time the movers had left there was a fire burning in the little back room which was to be Jack's study. His books were in order on the shelves.

"It looks as though you'd been living here for months," Ann remarked.

We stood for a moment in front of the house, resting after the long day. Tony was knee deep in yellow leaves. Across the road, wide autumn fields sloped to a far line of woods.

Jack said, "I feel, rather, as though I had been here not for months but all my life."

I put out my hand to touch the newel post on the fence, smooth as a ball in my palm, assuring myself that all this was real. After the years of war and all the waiting, the perfect end. And also, of course, the beginning.

Jack is an amateur photographer of some talent. Hence we have a visual record of our past. So we can reconstruct that year. The Hitchcock chairs, bought at auction; the white collie puppy, Jeff, who was to be a part of the family for the next fifteen years; the new station wagon. And most of all, Tony.

He was never still, never silent. His eyes had a life of their own, searching and alert. During the first month, with so much to be done in the new house, he followed me from room to room.

"Pretty," he would say of a book, or an ashtray, or a bright pillow. He would put his hand out and stroke it. "Tony likes dat."

He spoke in full sentences very clearly and very early. Like all young parents, we thought he was most unusual and were at the same time amused at ourselves for our foolish pride. Yet, after we had had three more chldren and were more experienced, we realized that Tony had in fact been unusual.

He had a keen awareness of beauty before he was even two years old. I recall, for instance, one winter afternoon when a fierce, fiery sunset filled the sky. Tony was standing on the sofa at the window, watching the cars go by, one of his favorite occupations.

"See," he cried, "see!" I came over to see what the excitement was about. He was jumping in his eagerness. "Fire," he cried, pointing to the sky, "fire!"

I thought he was unusually alert for his age and Jack said I was right. Tony could repeat a nursery rhyme after it had been said once. I can see him still, holding a huge volume of Mother Goose on his knees, pretending to read aloud as he turned the pages: "Simple Simon met a pie-man; Humpty Dumpty sat on the wall."

We were companions, Tony and I, during all that first winter on the farm, while Jack went about the job of settling himself into the new routine. Perhaps he and I were together too much: I have been told that we were. In any case, there was nothing else we could do. The days went by, the long house-bound days with an occasional excursion across the frozen fields on the sled and the drive to town once or twice a week for marketing or errands. I did not mind the confinement at all; I was pregnant again and did not have too much energy.

I did, though, have energy for painting and plenty of time to do it while Tony took his nap. I felt, without knowing how or why, that I was improving; a style which was entirely my own seemed to have developed without conscious effort. I painted boldly: simple objects, the rain barrel at the corner of the barn, apples in a wooden trough. I did a picture of the cat on the windowsill for Tony and he was delighted with it: an appreciative critic.

The quiet routine was enough for me. I was happy. And Tony was happy too, as long as the routine was unbroken.

The one thing he could not tolerate was being alone or with anyone else except me. On Saturday nights Jack and I always tried to get out, to visit new friends or even to see a movie. We had a fairly close neighbor, a middle-aged widow named Hanna Alcorn, who used to come to stay with Tony. She was a cheerful woman who had had several children, now grown. She seemed to be a perfect sitter for Tony.

But I remember him now, standing in the doorway, framed in the light and struggling to follow us while Hanna held on to him.

"Mommy, don't go! Don't go!" There was something so desperate about his cry it haunted me whenever we went out.

Then he did not want to be with other children. Sometimes one of our friends would call, bringing a child of Tony's age. But Tony never was glad to see him. He would cling to my skirt or climb on my lap, leaving his guest to play by himself.

I thought, He is shy and he will outgrow it. I recalled my mother's tales about my having been a "bashful" child myself. For that matter, neither Jack nor I was especially extroverted even then.

About a month before the second baby was due, my father had a heart attack. I left for Ohio at once. Hanna offered to stay until I could return. "Don't worry about Tony," she reassured me. "We'll have a good time together."

But the last thing I remember as Jack drove me to the station was Tony's pitiful cry: "Mommy, don't go."

Father died on the third day after I arrived. Jack came for the funeral and then returned home alone. I stayed another week to help my mother with all the sad, inevitable chores that accompany a death.

Tony was strained and quiet when I got back. Jack said that children of his age had no conception of time and my absence must have seemed forever to him. I had been home about two weeks when I had to leave again, this time to go to the hospital to have Jane. We had been preparing Tony in the approved modern manner for the arrival of the new baby, letting it be known that this was to be "his" baby, that he was going to help Mommy take care of it. He and I had even practiced giving the baby a bath with a doll from the five-and-ten.

"Come see what we have for you!" Jack called, when we came home from the hospital with Jane.

Tony came down the stairs slowly, clinging to Hanna's hand.

I pulled the blanket back so that he might see the little head in the pink, ruffled cap. "This is the baby we promised you, Tony. The one you were going to help feed, remember? And now here's something else." We showed him a beautiful, blue plush dog.

Jack put the dog into Tony's arms. "What are you going to call the doggie?"

Tony did not answer. He hung his head with his thumb in his mouth. He looked so lonely, so bereft, that I handed the infant to Hanna and asked if she would undress her. "Tony and I are going to take care of the doggie."

I reached out to take him on my lap but he pushed me back, flung the new dog away and threw himself on the floor in a burst of weeping that we could not quiet for half an hour. When at last we had soothed him, fed him and put him to bed, I was exhausted.

"He's just jealous of the baby," Hanna said reassuringly.

"I know, sibling rivalry. But it seemed so violent."

"He'll get over it," Jack assured me. "Don't take it so seriously." He patted my hand. "You've had a rough time in this last month." He turned to Hanna and told her how glad he was she could stay awhile, "It means a lot to me to know that you'll be here while I'm gone all day."

"I'll stay as long as you need me," Hanna said. Little did any of us know how many years we would need her!

Jane fitted right into the family; Hanna remarked that you hardly knew there was a baby in the house. She ate, slept and played on schedule. When she cried it was for a definite reason: she was hungry or wet. As soon as her needs were taken care of, she quieted. On warm afternoons we used to put her carriage out under a tree by the back door. We could hear her cooing as she amused herself with a toy dangling on a ribbon from the hood.

Not one to make comparisons, I could scarcely help realizing how different she was from her brother.

He did not get used to her. As the months passed his resentment of her seemed to grow. He was not yet in his third year and very articulate.

"Take that baby back to the hospital where you got her!" he commanded. "I hate her!"

Of course, that was only baby talk ... But really he did seem to hate her. After we caught him pounding her on the head with one of his blocks we made sure to keep her out of his reach. Jack put a hook high up on the door of Jane's room.

Hanna went home for a while and I was alone with the two children all day. I tried to give Tony enough time alone with me so that he would not feel displaced by the baby. I know I did these things because, years later, my brother-in-law reminded me of them.

"Do you know what you used to tell Ann and me every time we came to visit? You used to tell us not to pay much attention to the baby because it would upset Tony."

I had forgotten that. But I do know that both Jack and I sensed some deep hurt in Tony, and without seeing it as anything other than the heartache of a sensitive child who feels displaced we made every effort to assuage it. It took a lot of assuaging. Tony began to want me in sight every minute. He would follow me to the bathroom and pound on the door until I came out. When I talked on the telephone he would lie on the floor and cry for attention.

Bedtime became an ordeal. Jack would try to help me through this most difficult time of day, especially after Jane began to walk, and she walked at ten months. I had to get her bathed, fed and into bed, then get dinner on the table for Jack, and then get Tony to bed. But he never wanted to go. He was so active all day, literally never still for a moment, that one would have expected him to be eager for sleep, especially since he no longer took a nap. But he was wide awake.

Downstairs, trying to eat a quiet dinner, we would hear his piteous cries: "Mommy, come up! Come up!"

We decided to forget the rules. We would put off his bedtime. Surely he would be sleepy in another hour or two. Instead we found he could stay up until midnight. That, of course, we could not permit.

So we struggled through story-telling and rocking to get him somehow to sleep. And afterward, we would tiptoe down the stairs, praying that the telephone and doorbell would not ring to wake him again.

So slowly, so insidiously does one become accustomed to the most trying routine, that only recently did I recall how Jack used to telephone from town to ask: "How is he today?" Only now do I understand the enormous significance that such a question should be asked about a child, barely three years old.

3

WE decided to give up the farm. There was a tremendous shortage of doctors after the war, and Jack was as busy by the second year as he had hoped to be after five years. The farm admittedly was not the most convenient location; a seven-mile drive over a narrow road at three in the morning to operate on a ruptured appendix was not the easiest way to practice.

So we reasoned with each other. But the truth is, such emergencies were not that frequent. The farm with its space and peace was what we had both wanted all our lives and was worth any inconvenience. We did not want to leave, but in some vague way we thought we might do better for Tony. Perhaps the farm was not the place where he could be most happy, most "adjusted." Although we could not have known it then, we had already begun the long search for conditions that would be best for Tony.

We found a house in town, not far from the office and the hospital, pleasantly surrounded by an ample old-fashioned yard. The school was a healthy walk away. The roof was tight, the price reasonable. It was a large, drafty house with wooden gingerbread adornments but it had nooks where a boy might keep his trains and a girl her dollhouse. It had a wonderful, tall room, facing north, which would provide me with a real studio of my own. A family could spread out in that house and grow in comfort.

Jane was a year and a half when we moved. She was tall and lanky with the red hair and freckles of my family after a skip of two generations. Then as now she had none of Tony's beauty. But she had a kind of inner merriment that already drew people to her. Hanna loved her. Really, I think it was in part because of Jane that Hanna offered to come with us permanently. She could have got easier positions with childless families; she was a good cook and a real homemaker. But having decided to sell her old house now that her family had moved away, she elected to move into town and stay with us.

How glad I was to have her! We had been in the house not quite a year, had barely got painted, curtained and furnished, when the twins were born. They were a boy and girl, entirely different from either Tony or Jane. We named them Sarah and Freddy and decided that our family was complete.

Tony did not object to them as he had to Jane. He even seemed somewhat interested when Jack told him that someday he would have a lot of good times with his new brother.

I hoped so. Silently I hoped that a brother

would do for him what no other companion had
yet been able to do.

For the move to town had made no difference;
he still followed me around and clung to me.
There was a little boy of his age down the street. I
went out of my way to walk past Kevin's house
and to make friends with his mother. We arranged
to have the children exchange visits. But Tony
never wanted to be left at Kevin's house, so it fell
to Kevin to come to our house. Thus I was able to
observe for myself what happened.

The boys used to play in the sandbox and
things always ended in tears. Tony would come
weeping to Hanna or me.

"Kevin hit me."

"Well then, you must just hit him back."

"He took my shovel."

"You mustn't let him unless you *want* to give
it to him. It belongs to you."

I went outside and with the proper nursery-
school approach spoke reasonably to the boys.
"People don't ever take things. They *ask* for
them. Besides, you do have enough pails and shov-
els to go around."

Kevin always nodded wisely but then the same
thing would happen all over again. Kevin was a
perfectly nice little boy, no more belligerent than
any other little boy of four. He just enjoyed a
good wholesome fight now and then.

But Tony did not fight or could not. He was
afraid. The only child he was not afraid of was his
sister, Jane.

She loved company, any company, including
Tony's. They would play together for fifteen or

twenty minutes at a time, outside in the sandbox
or indoors building with their blocks. But invaria-
bly this play always ended in turmoil; the sight of
Jane walking freely across any open stretch seemed
to tempt Tony to knock her down.

After she had been soothed and comforted I
would turn to him.

"Tony, why did you knock Jane down again?
Why do you always make her cry?"

"I hate her."

"But you're the big brother," Hanna said. "You
must take care of her. Only bad boys knock their
little sisters down."

I had read the articles—who had not, in those
days when every woman's magazine and radio program for women spread the message of the new
psychology? Hanna, old-fashioned, small-town
Hanna, would sniff and tell me the way she had
brought up her own sons and her mother had
brought up six:

"It's all common sense. He ought to have the
daylight whopped out of him."

"That never helps," I argued.

"He ought to be knocked down himself, to see
how it feels."

I tried to talk to Tony. "I know sometimes you
hate Jane. I know sometimes you feel angry with
her. It isn't bad to feel that way, but it is bad to
hurt people and I can't let you do it."

"Stop reasoning so much with the boy," Jack
upbraided me. "I don't want to embarrass you in
front of Hanna, but privately I think she's right.
The next time he hurts Jane, give him a good
smack."

It was not hard to follow that advice. I was tired out; I had twin infants to feed and diaper and get up for at night. I had Jane who was barely out of diapers herself, and now this hyperactive, troublesome little boy.

So the next time he made me frantic with frustration I spanked him. It did no good. Tony went his own way and seemed to learn nothing either from punishment or from sweet reason.

One day he pushed Jane onto a stone step and drove her teeth through her lips. I was determined to have advice. I knew that Tony was beyond my control, that I was not handling him well and must be doing something wrong.

In that area, in those days, there was no child-guidance clinic or psychiatrist. But our pediatrician was a well-trained young man and he listened thoughtfully.

"Let's face it, some children are just more ornery than others," he said. "There's nothing so unusual about this situation. Tony is jealous of his sister, he's especially strong-willed—"

"He does exactly what he pleases," I said. "His answer is 'Because I want to' or 'You can't make me.'"

"You know," the doctor said, "a trait like that, however hard it is to live with at this stage of life, can be a great asset when properly directed. Tony looks like the kind of child who is always going to know exactly what he wants and will drive toward it with all his energies. Those are the achievers of this earth." He smiled.

I smiled too. This was a bit encouraging. "But how shall I handle him now?"

"Well, try to avoid situations. Be a little clever when you see them coming and circumvent them. Keep him and his sister apart when there is no one with them, for instance; then you won't have to make the choice of whether to handle him sternly or forbearingly. How you handle things depends so much on your mood of the moment anyway, doesn't it?"

That was true. When I was up all night I was more inclined to yell at Tony or spank him. When I was rested I was more inclined to sit down and say, "Let's talk this over and find out why you're so angry." Not very consistent, I knew.

"Inconsistent *and* human. Don't expect too much of yourself. You know, I was speaking to your husband in the coffee shop at the hospital yesterday and, frankly, I'm inclined to agree with him that you are making a perfectly understandable mistake that so many young mothers make: you're taking all this too seriously."

"I suppose so. But you want everything to be right. You want the family to be happy."

"Of course you do, and it will be, but no family is constantly happy anyway. Besides, time will take care of most of this. Tony will be in kindergarten before you know it and he'll have companions, an outlet for all that excess energy."

I began to feel much better. "Another thing," the doctor went on. "Jane will grow, too. She'll learn to handle herself. She'll fight back and it won't be so one-sided."

All this made sense. I don't know whether it was the reassurance and the rise in my confidence, but actually, for a while, things did begin to seem better.

Jane grew from babyhood into an extraordinarily independent child. It was strange to see how in one way Tony scorned and abused her and, in another way, relied on her.

I remember, for instance, the time Jack and I took the children to the circus. Tony wanted candy from a vendor a little distance away; I gave him some coins and he started off. He went a few steps, stopped and turned back.

"You ask the man, Jane," he said.

While we watched in astonishment, the three-year-old trotted over to the candy stand, made her selection and came back with candy for herself and her brother.

Such a complicated, puzzling little boy! And in so many ways, such a dear little boy! He had gentle, loving thoughts: saving pennies to buy a tie for Jack's birthday or putting a clumsy handful of zinnias on my desk. And he was so earnest, so full of questions.

"Sometimes I look up at the sky, and I wonder what my ancestors think of me when they look down."

He liked to go to the hospital with Jack on Sunday morning. Many of the doctors used to bring their children for Sunday rounds and keep them downstairs in the lobby.

"It's funny," Jack said, troubled. "He never talks. I feel sort of embarrassed. All the other men's kids talk away, while he just stands there clinging to me. He seems scared to death." Yet every Sunday Tony looked forward to going and Jack always took him.

It is such a mixed time, so hard to recall. Only in pictures does it come sharply to life . . .

I have photographs of that summer in Cape Cod when my mother joined us. There we are, three generations caught for an instant: the grandmother with the twins overflowing her lap, the parents with their hair blowing in the wind, the children standing before the salt-stained boards of the porch.

Then, home again, there is Jack standing at the barbecue in a chef's hat, handing hamburgers to Tony and Jane; there is a bag of potato chips on the table; it must have been a Sunday afternoon. And Jane with a doll carriage as large as herself. Here is Jack on the steps of the hospital; that must have been the day he was made chief of his own surgical service and he looks embarrassed at having his picture taken. Here we are dressed for Easter. What a beautiful hat I am wearing! I remember it well, cream straw with cornflowers. Tony is dressed up too, holding my hand, and, as always, one is surprised at the charm of his enormous eyes. Here is Tony again in a Hallowe'en suit printed like a skeleton, with a paper bag of candy clutched in his hand. There is something terribly moving about that childhood picture, of a little boy like millions of other little boys, while none of us has any foreknowledge of what is to become of him.

When I look at these pictures, and I seldom do, it seems as though I loved him more keenly than my other children, although I know that is really not so. The difference is that my love for this child was touched with a kind of pain. Think of it this way, the history of Tony: a long road, stretching from the first day. In the beginning it runs level and smoothly enough; soon it tilts a little downward, levels out again, tilts again downward, more sharply this time, toward the final plunge. Traveling this road, you are at first unaware of the angle of descent. Only after a long time, after looking backward, can you see how far you have dropped.

"You know," I told the kindergarten teacher, "quite by accident I have discovered that the surest way to get Tony to do anything is to tell him to do the opposite. When I am in a hurry and really have to get something accomplished, like putting his shoes on, I tell him not to do it and he puts them on, one two three."

"Oh, but you must never do that!" Miss Watts rebuked me. "In doing that you are telling him that reality isn't real. You can cause irreparable harm!"

We were sitting in the big kindergarten room, quiet after school hours, having a routine parent-teacher conference. Miss Watts was one of those remarkable spinsters whom one sometimes finds in the teaching profession, a woman who knows how to be a mother.

"Your little boy is not a secure or happy child," she said now, quite gently. "But I suppose you have been thinking about that yourself."

I explained as clearly as I could my muddled feelings about Tony. "He hates to go to school. I have a feeling he is afraid."

"He is afraid, yes. On the playground he stands close to me, trying to hold my hand. Tell me, what does your husband do with Tony? You've told me about your days with him, but what about his father?"

"My husband is gone for long hours," I responded. "He leaves before Tony is awake and can get home any time from six to nine. We never know. He isn't home at five like a man with an ordinary job."

"Well, the amount of time spent with a child isn't as important as the quality of the time. It's important for the boy at this age to make a transition from his mother to his father. Your husband must do things with Tony."

"We understand that. At night, Jack often reads a bedtime story while I put the babies to bed. And when Jack has to go over to the county hospital for consultation, he'll take Tony and they'll stop off at a farm and look at the animals. It's a nice ride and—"

"That's not quite what I had in mind. They ought to do masculine things. Like building with hammer and nails, say. And no women around."

With a pang I thought back to the farm. There that sort of relationship would come naturally; in the kind of life we now led, I explained, it was very difficult.

"Still we have to try."

On the way home I could see the sense in what Miss Watts said; at the same time I had a feeling her advice was somewhat contrived. That was always the way with me, this seeing both sides. Jack didn't like to do carpentry. For one thing, he had to be careful of his hands, but basically he wasn't the home handyman type.

I had to think of something else they could do together. Paint, perhaps? We had planned to have a handyman come in to paint the fence around the yard. Perhaps Jack and Tony could do it instead.

On Saturday Jack came home at three o'clock. It was supposed to be his "half day" but it never worked out that way. I saw at once that he was tired and would have liked nothing more than to sit down and put his feet up. However, he had promised to try painting. Not, I knew, because he especially believed in it, but he thought I did and wanted to reassure me. That was Jack.

We gave Tony one brush and Jack took his and they set to. I watched from the kitchen window. It looked homey, peaceful—yet somehow not quite right. And then my eye happened to wander across the street. I saw a group of neighborhood boys, playing together happily. Two children in Tony's own kindergarten class were laughing and roughhousing as they scrapped over an express wagon.

The next few days again I tried to lure boys into the house with cookies and picnic lunches, in hopes that on Tony's home ground they might become friends. They came willingly enough; they had a wonderful time playing with Tony's toys— while he went off alone or followed me around the house, begging me to read to him.

Soon he was in the first grade and the second. "The children don't like Tony," I complained. "What does he do? Can you understand why?"

"He rebuffs them," I was told. "He stands apart and they sense his fear of them. It's the old pecking order, you know. They sense immediately when a child is timid or in some way different and they make him suffer, either by tormenting or ignoring him."

The second-grade teacher was not as tactful as Miss Watts had been. "There has to be something wrong at home. All such trouble starts in the home," she said authoritatively.

"I don't understand how," I said.

"You need to give him more time. The trouble today is that people are too busy to spend time with their children."

"That's not true in our house!" I interrupted with some indignation. Apparently every teacher set herself up as a psychologist nowadays. "We have a very quiet social life; my husband wouldn't have time for a busy one even if we wanted it. When he's not working, he's home, and I'm home all the time. I have a five-year-old girl and three-year-old twins. Believe me, I don't have an extra minute. I'm a kind of amateur artist and don't even have time for that any more, though it means a great deal to me."

"Then you probably don't have enough time for Tony either. Because of the three younger children?"

"Maybe that's it," I said, suddenly too tired to protest. Actually Tony had more of my time than the other three combined.

Jane was now in kindergarten and had a group of friends in the neighborhood. When home she would adopt an amusing motherly manner toward the twins, gently fussing over them. These two were a lively pair quite attached to one another, who fought and made up without rancor. The three children were really quite self-sufficient, contented with such time I could give them at my convenience and with a bedtime story or two from Jack or me.

It was Tony who filled my hours. He had never fully outgrown his sleeping difficulty, so his demand for companionship and attention extended far into the night.

I remember one weekend when Jack's brother Russell and his wife came to visit. We had invited a few people in for dinner. I had flown about all day getting everything polished, arranging flowers, baking a cake. It was our first social evening in many months. Tony ruined it.

He came downstairs in his pajamas, grabbed food from the table and refused impudently to leave when Jack ordered him to do so. I could see Jack's rising anger and his effort to keep from losing his temper. I could read the disapproval on my sister-in-law's face. I had heard she thought Tony was horribly spoiled; tonight it surely looked as though she were right.

I got up firmly from the table and took Tony's hand. "You're coming upstairs with me. And no nonsense."

He went willingly enough but once up in his room refused to let me go. I realized that that was what he had wanted, to get me upstairs with him.

"Read me a story. Read *Robin Hood*."

"Tony, you are old enough to read your own

stories and I have guests. I'm going down-stairs."

"If you don't stay here," he said cunningly, "I'll do an Indian yell and wake up Freddy and Sarah. Then you'll really have a mess."

"Tony," I said, "if you don't behave I will take your new ball and bat away for a whole month."

"I don't care," he said; and he didn't. He never played with them.

I started down the stairs. Out of the corner of my eye I saw him dart toward Freddy's room. . . . For the sake of peace and propriety I spent the next hour in Tony's room reading to him. When at last he let me go and I went downstairs again, dinner was over and the guests were back in the living room. I sat down, my cheeks flushed.

They were discussing the son of a well-known family in town. It was a very "good" family; the parents were friends of most of the people there and everyone was genuinely concerned about what was happening to the son. Apparently he had wrecked the car, charged outrageous bills and caused unending trouble.

One of the men remarked: "He's got a good father and a good mother. Ruth's my own cousin and I have a high regard for her, but the fact is that I must lay the blame at her door. She's just too soft." The discussion went on to how she used to plead for the boy whenever his father wanted to take a hard line. She had meant well, of course, but the results were her fault all the same. Too much mother, everybody agreed.

When we were alone that night Jack turned upon me in anger. "Well," he said, "I hope you're satisfied. You heard them talking about the Sayer boy. Wait another ten years and that's what you'll have! You aren't doing yourself or Tony any favor by letting him get away with murder!"

As every wife knows, always, always, when something goes wrong with the child, it's considered her fault. I was exhausted and put up no more than a weak defense. "He isn't getting away with murder."

"No? What do you call this kind of thing? He domineers you, he tries to run the house. Almost eight years old and we can't even have a few guests in peace! Well, I don't intend to stand for it any more. I'm taking a firm hand in this and you stay out of it."

I was confused in my feelings. Still I felt I had some glimmering of truth. "It's not that I think he ought never to be punished," I said. "It's just that I think we ought to find the reason for his behaving this way in the first place. If we could find the reason, we could prevent such behavior in the future, don't you see?"

"Yes. Well, you go off hunting the reason while he makes a shambles of the house. I'm tired and I'm going to bed. But if he makes any more disturbance tonight, I warn you I'll spank the tar out of him."

I was desperate. "Jack," I pleaded, "listen to me. Maybe I have spoiled Tony; maybe I'm not the best disciplinarian. But if that's so, then I spoil all our children because that's the kind of person I happen to be. Why aren't they a problem? No, I don't believe that 'spoiling' makes Tony act the way he does."

"What does, then?"

"Tony isn't bad; he is telling us in his own way that he's miserable."

When he saw my distress, Jack's anger cooled. He wanted to know why Tony should be miserable in the first place.

"That's just it. I don't know."

Then I came out with what had been troubling me all evening long: "I know you don't think it's necessary, but please, let's get some advice. I want to take Tony to a psychiatrist."

At first Jack couldn't see it at all. He thought all Tony needed was some old-fashioned firmness. But I persisted and finally he acquiesced. "If you feel the need for reassurance, to set your mind at rest I'll make some inquiries in the morning."

At that time the nearest qualified psychiatrist was half a day's drive away. Jack arranged to take two days away from his office so that the doctor could have ample time to interview us and examine Tony.

We explained to Tony that he was to have some new kind of tests for school. He was quite satisfied, since anything to do with books or ideas appealed to him.

While several psychologists from the staff spoke to Tony, Jack and I spent half an hour with the doctor, relating the problem as we saw it. He was a small bald man with a dry manner and no smile. He asked very few questions, just watched us steadily, tipped back in his chair. When he was finished with us, we waited several hours more for Tony to get finished.

Since it would take them a full day to arrive at

their findings, we took Tony to the zoo and then out to dinner. He was immensely pleased to have us to himself. It was one of his good days. He had a lot to say about the animals; he knew their names, their habitats, their histories. He had a photographic memory and tremendous intellectual curiosity. He was so agreeable, walking along through the park between us, that we began to wonder whether we were imagining our trouble with him, whether our trip had been unnecessary. Next day we returned to the doctor, sure he would tell us we really had no problem worth talking about.

Tony was left in the waiting room in charge of a nurse while we went in to the doctor.

He began abruptly: "There is really nothing wrong with your boy." Of course! "I have the reports here and we have just had a conference about him. He does have some internalized conflicts; for example, his drawings indicate that he is extremely unsure of his own masculinity. But a few months of concentrated work with him will straighten that out with no problem at all."

I saw Jack's mouth forming a question, but the doctor went on. "The problem, as always, is not the child. It is the parents. But you must have known that," he said to Jack. "Primarily the problem is the mother, although the father is by no means without responsibility. For that reason, I always suggest psychotherapy for both parents, with two different therapists, of course."

My hands began to sweat—from guilt, shame, fear? I do not know. But I sat there, cold, with the inner trembling that was to be a part of me for many years.

"If either one of you wishes to come to this office, I will be glad to accept you in treatment and to recommend a colleague for the other. If you wish to make your own choice of two other men, you may certainly do that."

"I don't understand," Jack said. "Could you possibly give us any idea of what has led you to this conclusion, some clue as to what you see is wrong with us?"

Now at last, there was a smile, very small, very tolerant. "Well, doctor, that's not something you can unearth in a few minutes. That is why we are going to need a great deal of time to find out. This isn't like surgery, with a predictable time-table for recovery," he concluded, rather patronizingly.

"I understand that," Jack said. "All I am trying to ask is whether we, my wife and I, can be so greatly at fault that we have made Tony as upset as he seems to be. After all, we have three other children and they are getting along very well."

"Your attitudes toward the others may be—undoubtedly are—entirely different. They have no relevance to this child at all. This child may well be the focus of your own sickness."

"Doctor," I said, "I may as well tell you that coming here was my idea. I felt, I still feel, that I—we—need direction in bringing up Tony. I admit I do not understand him as well as I should, or perhaps at all, but what you are saying, if I understand correctly, is that my husband and I are sick people—"

"That is, of course, a matter of degree. You are obviously not crucially ill, because you are functioning in your respective roles. But then, a great many sick people do. One might say that you are able to walk, although you may be lame. Certainly you are not *well*. If you were, you would not be here with your child."

"And so it is we who have made Tony what he is?"

"Let me put it this way. Every child born, every mind, is a *tabula rasa*, an empty slate. What is written on it"—a stubby finger shot out, pointed at me—*"you* wrote there."

How long the stunned silence lasted, I do not know. But the nurse put her head in the door, saying in a loud whisper, "Tony is getting quite impatient. I really don't think that I—"

The doctor rose. "Tell him that his parents will be right out." Then to us: "I hope I've made myself clear?"

"Oh yes," Jack answered. "Quite." Only I could know the real meaning of his clipped, courteous manner.

"Think about it. Everything isn't hopeless, you know." Handshakes propelled us toward the door and for the first time there was a slight attempt at friendliness in the manner. "In two or three years we shall have got at the root of the affair. Call us after you've thought it over."

"We'll do that. Thank you," Jack said. And we gathered up Tony, who was in a temper from boredom.

Since we could not discuss our thoughts in front of Tony we rode home in silence, arriving near midnight to a sleeping household.

Finally, alone in our room we confronted each

other. "Well," Jack demanded, "do you still want to go to a psychiatrist?"

"Not that one. I loathed him."

"Why? Because he put the blame on you?" That was one of Jack's strong qualities; he could be incisively fair and objective even when his emotions were painfully involved. Tonight it was infuriating.

"No. Yes. I don't know. He was so sure about us! But he doesn't know anything about us! He spent only half an hour with us. How could he be so sure?"

"It's a theory," Jack said. "The current theory. It doesn't make sense to me, but then who am I to refute it? I admit I don't know anything."

"It's stupid!" My frustration sprang out in fury. "To think that I pinned my hopes on this! He didn't help us at all. I thought surely he'd have some definite advice about handling the child!"

"Would you be willing to undergo treatment yourself?"

"Yes, if you thought it made sense. But—"

"I've told you that I honestly don't think so. I don't see anything so peculiar about us. Not more than most people, anyway," he said with a wry laugh. "But then, I may well be wrong. Certainly *I'm* not insulted by the idea."

"And you mean that I am insulted?"

"You act that way. If there's anything I despise, Louise, it's false pride. You aren't above criticism, you know."

"I never said I was! This isn't a question of pride! I went to that man for advice. I was honest enough to admit that I needed direction, that

Tony is a problem to me; I asked for help. I didn't ask to be told I was crazy."

"He didn't say you were 'crazy.' "

"Now you're sounding like him. You, who had to be forced to go! Remember, I know your opinion of psychiatrists. You've expressed it often enough!"

"I won't deny that I've said harsh things about psychiatrists, that I don't think they are scientists, and a lot of them are fakes. But at least I'll admit they can see some things I can't, if only because they come in contact with these problems by the hundreds and I don't. As a matter of fact, maybe there is something wrong with you, you certainly do mollycoddle the boy. Every time I come home, I find you reading to Tony, sitting on the porch swing talking to Tony, placating him, *buying* the peace of the household! Why, are you afraid of him?"

"What do you want me to do, cane him if he doesn't stand at attention? He's eight years old, for heaven's sake! Why don't you stay home, and see whether you can do any better?"

I glared at him, hating him at that moment, hating him for not helping me, even for having fathered this child who was wearing me out.

Then suddenly as it had come, my anger was gone and there were only fear and a desperate need for comfort. We were like two strangers, blaming each other because we were so frustrated and afraid. "We have such a long way to go," I said at last. "We mustn't let this trouble turn us against each other."

For a long minute he looked at me, his eyes

troubled and sad. Then he put his arms around me. "Louise, I'm sorry. But his thing has grown until it's larger than life. Yet truly, I don't believe there is anything in what that man said. If I did I would go back willingly. I do believe there's nothing wrong with Tony except he's tense and high-strung. And we are too, because we take everything too seriously. So he comes by it naturally. Let's just settle down and cultivate a sense of humor and live through his growing pains. I'll try and do my share and we'll work this out together."

Relief poured over me. This strong, good man was not only my husband but a doctor of great skill. Surely he was more to be depended upon than the arrogant, chilly little man we had seen that morning! Hope, which had been high earlier in the day and had been dashed brutally to pieces, came surging back . . .

In later years I was to think: perhaps we ought to have followed the doctor's advice whether we liked him or not. Maybe if he had been less arrogant and abrupt, more tactful, more kind, we would have done so. Or if he had not been so many miles away and the whole business such a stupendous physical undertaking. Who can tell? But we resolved to manage for ourselves, confident in our own good intentions, our courage, love and common sense.

Thus we were able to manage for three more years, and then when Tony was eleven the crash came.

4

WE had no warning of how bad it would be. In fact, for a year or two before it came Tony seemed to be better; I thought I saw a kind of settling process. In fifth grade he was in an advanced section for gifted children. He had a great deal of work to do, but he did it without complaint. He never had to be reminded to do his homework, but went to his room and worked with tremendous zeal. He did not seem to be grinding. He read everything from Jules Verne and Mark Twain to the best science fiction and the Sunday New York *Times*. He wanted to know everything. He thought a good deal about world problems. He was too earnest for his years, worried about the fate of the starving hordes in India, about racial injustice and the Cold War. We had always been accustomed to letting the talk at the dinner table roam over whatever was happening in the world, but we began trying to keep to light subjects when we saw that Tony was so deeply concerned. There was almost no laughter in him at all. His life was school and the work he brought home.

I remember how he upbraided me because of the subjects I chose to paint. Now that I no longer had any infants I was able to make time for art. I had even begun to take lessons at an art colony a few miles out of town, and had won a third prize at the fall exhibit.

Tony thought that my prize-winning work was sentimental. Very likely it was; a girl on a swing with her white skirt floating above a miniature landscape.

"You ought to pay more attention to the real world," he scoffed. "You'll never be a really great artist anyway."

"That's true," I admitted. "I know that."

In one sense I was proud of Tony for having such astonishingly mature discernment. But in another, I was a little hurt. My work was truly not bad; I would have liked my son to be pleased with it.

So little pleased him. He still had no friends and that troubled us very much. Yet we knew that there have always been scholarly, introverted people who do not adjust well to others but manage to find places for themselves in the world and are content in their way. And, as I say, in some ways Tony did seem more content. The nights were no longer such turmoil, even though he still could not sleep well; sometimes his light would be on until midnight and no remonstration could make him turn it out. For that matter, you still could not make him do anything he did not want to do.

He had very little contact with the rest of the family. Sometimes he and Freddy played checkers together. Freddy soon learned to let Tony win because he became enraged when he was beaten. But more and more the rest of the family accepted his irritability and avoided him as much as possible. Besides, they all had busy lives of their own. Jane had a little crowd of girls who visited back and forth. She took dancing lessons and fancied herself a future prima ballerina. She was quite motherly toward Sarah, who, now that she was in the first grade, amused us by consulting her elder sister about dresses and coiffures.

Freddy lived in a private world of sport. I remember how we had looked forward to a rich relationship between brothers. Perhaps under other circumstances it would have come later. But Freddy at six was as different from Tony as anyone could be. He was a homely little fellow, somewhat loud and argumentative, well able to take care of himself on the block. Jack said he had a big mouth, but it was easy to see that the father was very pleased with this little boy. Freddy now paid only the most casual attention to his twin sister; he was entirely absorbed with trading baseball cards, marbles and guns. He certainly was not a reader; he never sat still long enough. It was sometimes hard to realize that when Tony had been six and had first learned about Lincoln's freeing the slaves he had been dreadfully upset by the whole concept of slavery. Freddy would neither have understood nor cared. How different Tony was, how exceptionally sensitive, how easily hurt!

Yet, I saw with uneasiness, Tony was very well able to inflict hurt on others. Or I thought I saw it—even today it is not entirely clear.

Tony had no interest in baseball except when his younger brother and the other six-year-olds were playing in our yard. Then he would come out, bringing his own bat and hard ball, to have these babies pitch to him, or to pitch to them. Jack first became aware of what was going on. Tony, who was exceptionally strong, was using all his strength in his pitches, which came dangerously close.

One day, in spite of his father's stern warning, he struck Freddy on the head.

When we came running outside, Tony was crying as hard as Freddy. Jack ran to examine Freddy and I put my arm around Tony to comfort him. "I know you didn't mean it," I told him.

"You'd better feel sorry for the six-year-old," Jack admonished angrily. "He could have lost an eye."

"You're right," I said meekly. "Tony, we've told you and told you not to play so hard! You're ten years old and so much bigger!"

"I didn't mean it," Tony kept saying. "I didn't mean it."

If only, I thought, he would go make some friends of his own age.

Then suddenly he told us he wanted to go to camp for the summer. Not very many boys in our area went to camp; those who did were gregarious and athletic. So we were surprised and very uncertain.

But my brother-in-law, Russell, was persuasive, as was Tony's teacher.

"It might be just the thing to take him out of his solitary habits," the teacher said when I consulted her. "Living for eight weeks in a cabin with a group of boys, he'll be bound to make at least one friend and that will carry over into the fall."

"It'll make a man of him," Russell assured us.

"How do we know he really wants to go?" Jack asked. "He might hate it."

"Then you can bring him home. Good heavens, you're not forcing him! The boy wants to go!"

That was certainly true. And you had to have some confidence in a child's own feelings about himself.

He did seem to want to go. He did a good deal of talking and boasting about it, especially to Freddy, as though he wanted to make him feel inferior. Yet I sensed that Tony was actually frightened. I kept the feeling to myself, however. When the day came to take him to the bus he was white-faced and quiet. Still, when we arrived at the terminal I noticed tears on two or three other boys' faces and concluded that Tony was not so different after all. We assured each other on the ride back home that this would be the best possible experience for him.

Summer that year was a high-running tide for our family. Ever since the war Jack had kept in touch with the hospital where he had had his surgical training. Not wanting to stagnate, he went regularly to conferences and clinics; he was a well-known figure there in spite of living in the next state. One day, the telephone rang with a startling offer. One of Jack's own professors wanted an associate: would Jack consider pulling up roots and coming to work with him? There would also be a teaching post in the medical school.

Jack was as excited as a boy. To work in a teaching hospital! To be at the heart of the medical world, where new things were happening! There could be no question about what Jack would do. I was so happy for him. And there would be so many advantages for the children, besides; better schools, concerts, all the activities of a university-centered life. Tony especially would thrive on it, I thought.

The summer was hectic. Once more there was a house to be sold and a new one found. This time we found a graceful white New England clapboard not far from the university, exactly what we wanted. We were able to move almost at once. Tony would come home from camp to his new house, and everyone would be ready for the new school and the new life in September.

So we were unable to see Tony until midsummer, after we had got the rest of the family settled. There were a few postcards: "Send me some peanut bars," or "We had a fried chicken picnic today." In short, they said nothing. But then, didn't all boys send such terse, cryptic messages from camp? We called the director to inquire about Tony and was told he was shy, a quiet boy, but he was getting along fine.

So with only normal anticipation we drove into camp one morning in late July. Tony was waiting for us in the parking field, sitting alone, on a boulder. He stood up slowly when we brought the car to a stop.

"How's the boy?" Jack cried.

"Fine," Tony said flatly.

"Really?" I said. "You really like it?"

Jack flashed a look at me. "Of course, why shouldn't he like it?"

Tony wanted to know if we had brought cherries and peanut bars.

"Everything you asked for and enough to feed a regiment besides. But come on, let's go off to your bunk and see what's going on."

"No," Tony said. "I want to sit in the car with you."

"Hungry?"

We climbed back into the car. Tony got in the front seat between us. *Homesick, poor little fellow. He wants to be near us.* I put my arm around his shoulder.

We opened the cardboard boxes. There were homemade butter cookies, Hanna's specialty; chocolate brownies, my specialty; cherries, half a dozen splendid peaches, candy. Tony began to eat, silently, methodically, voraciously.

"Hey!" Jack remonstrated. "You aren't going to eat your way through all that at once?"

"I'm hungry," Tony said stubbornly.

"You won't be able to move!" I cried gaily. But I felt a certain uneasiness I could not explain.

"Don't they feed you down here?" Jack inquired lightly.

"Yes."

Silence again except for Tony's chewing.

"Have you been on an overnight yet?"

"Yes."

"Where to?"

"The mountains."

The floor of the car was strewn with paper; peach juice had run down Tony's chin and stained his shirt. Still he kept eating.

"No more," Jack said, sharply now. "That's all for now. Come, take us to your cabin."

"I don't want to."

"Why not? What's the matter?"

"Nothing, I just don't want to."

"Tell us, Tony," I said. "Is there something wrong? Aren't you happy here?"

"Yes." The tone and his face were without expression.

"Well, then, let's go, we'll come back to the car later."

Jack and I got out and began walking down the path toward the center of camp.

Slowly Tony followed. At the cabin the other boys were cleaning up. We met the counselor, a friendly college sophomore, who led us down to the lakefront while Tony changed for swimming.

We took advantage of Tony's absence to talk to the counselor about him. "He's a nice kid," we were told. "I wish the whole lot were like him. He doesn't make a bit of trouble. Obeys all the rules, always on time, clean—"

"That's good to hear," I said. "But, tell me, is he having a good summer?"

"Oh, I think so. He *is* awfully quiet, hardly says anything. But I asked him last week whether he liked it here and he told me he does. So I guess it's just his way, a quiet type. Probably a great student, isn't he?"

"Yes, he is a good student."

"I thought so. In free time, instead of raising Cain with the others, he sits in his bunk and reads. Deep stuff for a kid his age. Oh, there's the gang! Sorry, I have to leave you, but look for me later on; we're having a baseball game to entertain the parents."

And he was off, a muscular, confident young man who meant well . . .

My uneasiness deepened. We were caught up in a crowd of arriving parents, some of whom we knew. There was much greeting and confusion. Lunch was a picnic buffet, with everyone milling around and Tony quiet at our elbow, still eating, going back for seconds. Where did he put it? How could he eat so much?

Next came the rest period, then the big event of the day, the baseball game. In the scramble of small boys around the benches and at home plate, Tony stood apart. Nobody spoke to him, nor did he speak to anyone. All at once, I saw him again on the playground of Miss Watts' kindergarten, watching the other children on the swings. Parents around us were caught up in the spirit: 'Mike's a great little pitcher, you ought to see the kid—"
"My boy does all right at baseball, but what he really is is a water rat. They just put him into advanced diving—"

The teams were straightening out, the basemen walking to their places. Tony was way out on the meadow. Where else do you put the dud? But he

was one of the *extra* outfielders; each team had
too many players and Tony had been placed in
what might be called "the outer outfield." We
could barely see him. The game dragged. Unless
your own son is a star, there are few events less
stimulating to a woman than a children's baseball
game. We stood for three or four innings, while
they changed teams, and each time Tony, predict-
ably, was struck out. He again trudged back to
the outfield, and had been there a while when Jack
asked me suddenly: "Where is Tony? I don't see
him any more."

"He must be there."

"Come on," Jack said. I followed him around
the diamond, through the high, shaggy grass to
the spot where Tony had been stationed.

We found him lying face down on the ground; I
do not know whether or not he had heard us
swishing through the grass but he did not stir. We
stood there a moment looking down at him and
then Jack spoke softly.

"Hello, son."

Tony looked up and slowly got to his knees.

"You better stand up, Tony. Suppose a fly ball
came sailing by?"

Tony nodded and stood all the way up.

"Bored out here? Is that it?"

"I don't like baseball."

"Well, all right. But I wouldn't do this again if
I were you. The fellows would be awfully sore at
you if you let a ball go by."

Tony nodded again. We heard a flurry of calls
and cries and saw the teams were changing sides.

We let Tony go and walked back slowly by ourselves.

I opened my mouth to speak. Then I saw Jack's set face and something told me to be still.

We left camp late that afternoon. In the parking field Jack asked Tony whether he wanted to stay for the rest of the season.

"I want to stay." The answer was toneless.

"You're sure?"

"I'm sure."

We kissed him good-by and he walked away. Then he came back and kissed us both again, an unusual display of affection for him.

"Good-by, Tony, see you in a month."

There was a long lane out to the main road. I looked back for as long as I could, and saw him standing there, a lonely figure with upraised arm, very small. We rode for a mile or so without speaking until I could hold back no longer.

"Jack, how do you think he is, really?"

"How?" Jack's voice roughened. "I'll tell you how. Tony is psychotic. Tony has schizophrenia."

I thought it was my husband who had lost his mind. "Jack, for God's sake, what are you saying? You can't know what you're saying!"

"Did you see him, lying there on the grass? Cut off from everyone. I saw it and I see the future as plainly as I have ever seen anything in my life."

My strength drained away. "Jack," I pleaded, "are you really making any sense at all? He's shy— granted. He's a poor athlete and he's afraid to play because other boys are always so contemptuous of a poor athlete. That's not at all unusual."

"This is different. The flat manner. The abnormal appetite. I'm aware I'm not qualified to diagnose, but it's something that, as a doctor, I *know*. God help me, I wish I didn't."

"Jack, with all respect to you, you're not a psychiatrist."

"Please," he said. "I know what I see."

He turned on the radio and began to drive very fast, which was not like him at all. I saw he did not want to talk. He looked strange, unfamiliar to me. I put my head back and thought: *No, he's wrong, he's got a tendency to be pessimistic anyhow. He admits he has. I will not listen to these graveyard thoughts.*

We did not mention the word "schizophrenia" again. I dismissed the whole thing as an emotional outburst, a father's hurt pride.

We were caught up the rest of that summer in the business of the new house. I readied Tony's room with special care: ample shelves for his many books; twin beds in the hope that he would invite a friend to stay overnight; and, as a homecoming present, a remarkable wooden brontosaurus to add to his collection of prehistoric animals.

The whole family went to meet the camp bus, three children, two dogs, Jack and I. Tony looked tan and strong. In the confusion of the car we could tell nothing, nor in the excitement at home, as the others pulled him around to show the new house, the yard, the playroom above the garage.

Later that night after all the children had gone to bed and Jack and I were reading on the porch, we heard sounds that sent us flying upstairs.

There, in the cheerful red and white plaid room, face down on the bed, lay Tony. His fists were clenched and he was pounding the pillow, crying in breathless, painful gasps.

Jack put his hand firmly on Tony's shoulder. "I'm here, son. What is it?"

The crying grew more intense. Jack motioned to me to leave the room. I went out and sat on the steps of the upstairs hall. After a long time the weeping died away; then there was only a murmur of voices and the hammering of my heart.

At last Jack came out, softly closing the door. We went into our own room.

"He begged me not to send him back to camp," Jack said. "Apparently he went through hell."

"What happened?"

"The boys tormented him. They wouldn't let him alone. They ganged up on him, put a snake in his bed, ants in his clothes." Jack was grim.

"That counselor!" I said, outraged. "He was hired to watch the children, to prevent just this sort of thing. He told us Tony was 'doing all right.' "

"I know. But he was only a kid. He didn't understand. You can't watch children every moment of the day. A boy of Tony's age ought to be able to take care of himself."

"That Mickey Lumus is such a bully! If only Tony hadn't been in his cabin—"

In the half darkness I could see Jack's face. "Louise, if it hadn't been Mickey, it would have been somebody else. Kids can always smell out the weak one and then they don't let him rest. It's cruel, but that's the way it is. The problem is Tony, not the other kids."

"Why didn't he tell us, why didn't he come home?"

"He has a lot of pride, for all his softness. He was afraid of what all these people would say if he was 'chicken.' So he stuck it out, poor fellow. Tomorrow," Jack said firmly, "I'll find out who is the best man for children. I guess it was fate that we moved here. At least, in this town, we'll be able to get the best psychiatric help available. For what it's worth," he concluded cryptically.

5

THE child who had gone away to camp had been, Heaven knew, nervous, irritable, and difficult, but at least he had functioned. Certainly we never would have allowed him to go, if we believed he would not go on functioning. The child who came back from camp was a ruin.

After the first day home I noticed that Tony was beginning to follow me around again, just as he used to do when he was a toddler on the farm. But now, the boy was almost as tall as I and his silent presence was troubling. He followed me to the kitchen, and stood there watching while I put cans on shelves. He followed me to the attic where I was hanging clothes in the storage closet. When I went to the bathroom I found him standing there waiting for me as I came out.

"Tony," I said, "Jane is going down to the hardware store for curtain rods. Would you like to go along and help her?"

"No."

"But you ought to get acquainted with the

neighborhood. You'll be starting school the week after next."

No response.

"Besides, she can't carry everything without some help."

"Why is she so tall?"

I didn't catch the question immediately, so that he had to repeat it.

Then I understand. Jane, our lanky redhead, had grown suddenly in the past year and was actually a fraction of an inch taller than Tony.

I answered lightly, "I suppose she takes after your Grandmother Howell's family. They were all tall, skinny redheads."

Jane laughed, but Tony demanded angrily, "Is she going to stay taller than I am?"

"Most likely not," I said. "It's too early to tell."

"Damn you, you'd better not be taller than I am or I'll knock your teeth out," he threatened her.

"Tony, don't be foolish; she can't help how tall she is. We all just have to accept the way we're made."

Tony moved toward his sister, his fist balled. "I said I'll knock her teeth out."

"Jane," I said hastily, "please go for the curtain rods. I need them now."

That night I spoke to Jack. "That thing you said the day we drove back from camp . . . do you still think Tony has—"

"Louise, I don't know; I'm all mixed up. Maybe I was hasty. At any rate, I got in touch with the head of the psychiatric department today. He was very encouraging, so maybe I was wrong. He said

Tony's young enough and that therapy at his age can do marvelous things. He recommended group therapy, said it's excellent for youngsters. There's a woman here who is very much sought after." Jack laughed grimly. "It seems you almost have to have pull to get an appointment. But I made it. You're to take Tony there on Friday at three-thirty."

I felt so relieved. I had heard they could do wonders. "Jack, I don't know why but I have a strong feeling that things will work out."

"Good; keep feeling that way."

Friday couldn't come fast enough. I went in first alone to see the doctor. She was a pleasant-looking young woman. Her office was surrounded by playrooms with everything in the way of equipment, from a dollhouse to a punching bag.

I started to tell, as briefly as I could, what our troubles were. After the first minute or two she interrupted me.

"All I really wanted was some facts about the family, number and ages of the other children and so forth. I would rather that you didn't tell me anything about Tony, or give me any of your opinions about him. That I shall find out for myself." She smiled encouragingly. "Now, if you'll step out, I'd like to see Tony."

I do not know what happened in the first therapy session, but I knew we were not to talk to him about it or do other than listen to anything he might tell us. Of course he said nothing. But after the third visit, he came out with a furious, flushed face. "I'm not going back! There's a girl there who was in my class at school. I'm not going to have her spread things about me all over the school."

I could understand his position. "I'll speak to the doctor," I promised. "Perhaps she can change you to another group."

"I won't go, anyway. I can't talk about anything in front of other kids. Besides, I haven't got anything to talk about."

"But, Tony," I said gently, "you have got things to talk about. You know you have."

"I'm not going to any psychiatrist! They're for nuts and I'm not a nut!"

"Tony, let me explain something. Psychiatrists are not for 'nuts'; they are for people who have things on their minds that are making them unhappy. Why, practically everybody at some time or other in his life has something that bothers him. And psychiatrists can straighten out their thinking, help them feel good again. That's all there is to it."

"I'm not going back there again," he insisted.

Jack agreed with me that perhaps we ought to make a change. "Anyway, I've been thinking that perhaps a man might be better. I'll ask around again tomorrow."

So we began our relationship with Dr. Gustaf Maxwell. He has a lofty reputation in the academic community, so many of whose children, it seemed, were undergoing analytic psychotherapy. Jack and I had the first interview without Tony. Jack described as succinctly as possible what the trouble was.

Dr. Maxwell was a neat, gray man with small steel-gray eyes behind steel-rimmed spectacles.

When Jack had finished the doctor turned to me. "Have you anything to add?"

"No," I said, "my husband has told you everything, except maybe that I would just like to add that I am so baffled by what has happened to our child. We have a good home, doctor. Believe me, we have."

"Why do you feel it necessary to tell me that? No one has said you haven't," he responded, quietly enough.

I was hotly embarrassed. "I mean," I explained, "that it might help you to know that Jack and I haven't got any problems between ourselves that would upset a child. We never fight—"

"You never fight?" he repeated.

I was tripped up, and tangled in my own words. "Not seriously, that is. . . ." I tried again. "I just mean there isn't any reason that I can see, nothing wrong with our home that would have made Tony so unhappy," I finished, annoyed with myself.

Dr. Maxwell looked steadily at me. "Nothing wrong that you are aware of. But no child is born with problems. It is always something in the home. In some way he has been damaged in your home."

The accusation fell into the quiet air like a stone into a pond and sank away.

"What can we do now?" I asked meekly.

"We shall uncover the stresses and work the situation through." Then, more kindly, "Nothing is irreparable, you know. As long as you are patient. It will take time."

We understood that. Certainly I did not like

this man, but we had not consulted him because I might like him, I knew.

"You talk too much," Jack exclaimed irritably as we drove home. "Why do you always have to confuse the issue with so much talk?"

I looked at him. And I realized he was not angry—he was afraid. "Oh, Jack," I said, "we're both so scared. Let's not take it out on each other!"

But of course, we did. A very difficult time began, made more so by outside circumstances which ordinarily would have been delightful. We were being welcomed, visited, invited on every side. The medical faculty, the P.T.A., the neighbors all extended themselves to us as newcomers. We were asked to serve on committees, to come to dinner, to the Friday musicale, to Sunday picnics. "Bring all the children," they said. But Tony never wanted to go, and since Hanna went out on Sunday what were we to do with him?

We could count on him now for a tumultuous disturbance about once every ten days. The rest of the time he was quiet, following the pattern of the last few years during which he had more or less retreated to his room and his books. The trouble was that we never knew when the outbreak would come or what would set it off.

Jane bothered Tony. Her height bothered him, her liveliness and the fact that, even here in a new community, the telephone kept ringing for her.

"What has Jane got that I haven't got?" he demanded one day.

I did not envy Jack the job of answering. "Oh, well, she likes people, and anyway, girls do grow up a little sooner, you know." He fumbled. "You'll catch up soon."

Tony stared at his father. And then he said distinctly: "You can drop dead."

"Tony!" I cried. "How can you say such a thing to your father?"

Jack whirled on me. "Stop it, Louise. I don't need you to defend me. I'll handle this myself."

Something was indeed happening to us. Jack had never been so sharp with me, so quick to snap at my most innocent remark. And the more he snapped, the more self-conscious I became. Sometimes it seemed I could feel the tension like a palpable thing in the house.

And life ought to have been so good. Jack was doing the work he really wanted. He had recognition, intellectual challenge and no financial problems. In the family, too, there was so much to be thankful for, if only we could have had peace in which to enjoy it.

Now almost eight, our twins were emerging abruptly from a noisy childhood and becoming individuals in their own right. Sarah had unmistakable musical talent. She was a dreamy, poetic sort of child with not nearly as many friends as Jane had, but she had a close group of two or three who kept her busy. She had her piano lessons, her daily hour of practicing and rehearsals for the school orchestra. Freddy developed, rapidly, a very distinctive personality. He even looked different from the others in the family, with a large nose and prominent ears. His black eyes snapped and sparkled. He had an alert expression, eager and curious about anything—a grasshopper, a carpenter driving

THIS STRANGER, MY SON   71

nails. Above all, he was so friendly. I often think
about him. There was nothing that anyone did to
make Freddy the way he was and is. He simply
arrived upon this earth like that, joined his family, the community of the street, the school and so
on, in ever-widening circles. He seemed to find
everything easy and possible, with no help from
anyone.

Inevitably, as Freddy became more assertive, he
ran head-on into Tony. He had unfortunately
overheard some talk about Tony's going to a psychiatrist and, as children will, soon gathered his
big brother was in some sort of trouble.

One rainy afternoon Freddy and two of his
friends were making a racket in the hall outside
Tony's room. Suddenly Tony's door was flung open
and from downstairs I could hear him bellow at
the younger boys, "Shut the hell up, or I'll beat
you."

Next I heard an Indian war whoop from Freddy, followed by the taunt, "Tony goes to the
psychiatrist! Tony goes to the psychiatrist!" Then
I heard the howl as Tony seized his brother and
flung him against the wall. I flew upstairs in time
to treat Freddy for a bloody nose. That is how we
began now to live.

Out of all the emotions of those months, the
bewilderments and fatigues, I recall most a dead
center of immobility in myself. Often I used to
stop and stand wherever I was, trying to think,
wishing I knew what to do, and which of all the
feelings that tore through me I ought to act
upon. At night, when finally the house was quiet,
I remember sitting in the old wing chair in my

bedroom, pulling myself and my thoughts together, trying not to cry, praying for enough strength to get through whatever lay ahead. I had a deep foreknowledge that what lay ahead was going to be very hard.

Most difficult to bear was our own ignorance. The doctor told us nothing. I understood that we were not dealing with anything that had a ready answer. Yet I wanted so badly to be told something, to have some general idea of where we stood.

After the first few weeks we were directed to take Tony to a psychologist for a battery of tests, the results of which were to be submitted to Dr. Maxwell. We were told that these tests were to evaluate Tony's basic intelligence and also to uncover his attitudes and conflicts. I did not ask for a complete report, since I knew quite well that I was not competent to understand or to evaluate it. But I did ask for some general information along understandable lines: how deep is the disturbance?

"There is no need for you to know," said Dr. Maxwell. "When there is need, I will tell you."

My contacts with him were few, a nod from the door of the waiting room on arrival and departure. Every other month I received a note giving me an appointment to visit him without Tony, at which times I was to report on what was happening at home.

After the first few visits my report was only repetition. "I have become an umpire in the house. Tony will not leave his brother and sisters alone. When Sarah has to practice the piano that's when he wants the piano to bang on, so he pushes her off the bench. When all three of the others are watching a program on television, he comes in, decides he wants something else and switches their program off. You can imagine what happens! To tell the truth, I'm afraid to leave the house any more except when Tony's at school. I'm almost afraid to leave the room."

Suddenly my tears rose, tears of frustration and fatigue. My embarrassment only made it worse. Furthermore, instead of turning away so that I could recover, the doctor continued to stare bluntly at me.

"Why are you crying?" he asked.

Didn't I have reason to cry? But no doubt he had a valid reason for asking. So I answered tearfully.

"Because I am terribly worried. I am tired out. You have no idea how hard it is to live like this. These last few months, it is as if the family were being torn apart. The other children say that Tony is crazy and they are beginning to hate him. . . ."

There was a long silence. These silences made me so uncomfortable. No, truly I did not like this man.

But did that not say something about me? Why didn't I like him? Because he made me feel it was I who was on trial, that all this . . . this *mess*, was my fault? He made me feel guilty. Indeed, I thought, as the silence ran humming in the compressed little room, I have things to feel guilty about. I yell at Tony; I lose my temper. I am not a good mother. I am not always patient, firm and kind as you are supposed to be. Always in control, mature; that's it, I am not mature.

"What is your father like?" the question whipped at me.

"My father is dead," I replied.

"What was he like?" The even voice persisted.

He wants to know your early conditioning toward men, to see how you may subconsciously feel toward your son, I thought, and then: *oh, don't be such a smart aleck.*

"I liked him," I answered slowly, searching for the truth. "He was a kind of blustering man at times, but he always got over his anger quickly and he was . . . well, I guess it's hard to sum up a human being, but he was *good*. He was cheerful and generous with himself. I liked him; I miss him still."

No clues there, apparently.

"I understand that you are an artist. Can you tell me something about that?"

"Well, yes, I paint. I've been studying at the university. I want to prepare a one-man show for next spring, but lately I haven't done much. I've been too upset about Tony."

"Why do you paint?"

I hesitated. Why did his questions always seem to harbor an accusation?

"I suppose simply because I like to. It's the same for everybody; I mean, it's the same as liking to play the violin or do anything—"

"You feel that it fills some need in you that nothing else fills?"

"No, that's not it. I'm satisfied with my role as

wife and mother, if that's what you mean." I hadn't meant to speak sharply and was afraid I had sounded sharp.

"I didn't say anything about your not being satisfied. You did." Dr. Maxwell spoke very quietly. I had to strain to hear him.

"A misunderstanding. I'm sorry."

Silence again. It seemed to me that this man was really inept, but who was I to judge? At any rate, I couldn't bear these silences, this feeling of getting nowhere.

"You see," I began deliberately, trying to get to specifics, "I have a feeling that we have no plan, no method. Jack and I don't agree on what to do with Tony, but then, neither one of us really knows, either. Yet we never have such doubts about our other children. I seem to know when they've done wrong and what to expect of them. With Tony, it is he who seems to be controlling me and always has. I feel," I said, "like a marionette, and Tony pulls my strings. Last week his teacher told me very tactfully that he ought to be wearing clean shirts to school." I glanced up at the impassive face and it flashed across my mind that he was thinking: Middle-class pride and status; she is afraid of what people will say because her son wears a dirty shirt.

I went on almost defiantly, "Yes, I do care. I was mortified. He goes down into the basement and takes a week-old shirt out of the pile of dirty clothes. Last Sunday the whole family was invited to a picnic and Tony came downstairs in torn dungarees and that same shirt. We had a terrible fight. When nothing else worked, Jack finally lost his temper and spanked him. Too hard, I think; it hurt me to see it but it was the only way we could make Tony change his clothes.

"I wish I had some rules or instructions to guide me. For instance, at night now, all of a sudden Tony has reverted to something he hasn't done in several years: I have to read him to sleep. He's almost twelve years old! I wouldn't mind if my reading gave him some security or answered some need. But the thing is, he won't let me finish. After every chapter he begs for one more, and after that, for one more. I've tried to see just how much he would accept if I were to give him all he wanted. The other night at eleven-thirty he still wasn't tired although my voice had almost gone. My husband came upstairs and was very angry and made me stop. He said it was ridiculous; that the child needed his sleep and besides he mustn't have his own way about everything. Also, that a man is entitled to his wife's company in the evening. And all that makes sense! The only thing is that when I do quite firmly get up and go out, Tony screams and screams and gets out of bed and wakes the other children. Then the house is in a turmoil and Jack is furious and spanks Tony, and it is just so horrible. So finally Tony goes to bed, sobbing, and that's surely no condition in which to end the day. Perhaps you could just give me some advice about how to handle things like that?"

The doctor made a pyramid out of his hands. He said deliberately, "There are no rules, you know. Nothing that I can give you in black on white."

"I know, but—"

"Understanding must come from within yourself. You must act upon your own feelings toward your child. You must have, spontaneously, the feelings that will tell you what to do."

I thought, If I had any other feelings besides confusion I wouldn't be in this predicament.

Tony went to Dr. Maxwell for one year. He got no better and he got no worse. Somehow we got through that year. We knew, of course, that the psychiatric process was lengthy, probing and painful. That it required an atmosphere of patience and optimism. We knew all that and we really tried. We gave every spare minute to Tony. I put my easel and paints away. Maybe, I thought, my painting *had* been some kind of escape from my obligations to my family. Dr. Maxwell must know something, after all. And anyway, I had no taste for painting now. Certainly, under our present circumstances, the one-man show was unthinkable, as were the lessons or the art history or anything else.

But I did begin to read extensively about emotional disturbance in children. Jack told me not to do so, quoting Pope to the effect that "a little learning is a dangerous thing." Yet this little learning would have been impossible to avoid even if I had tried to; in child-centered America, you are exposed daily to the subject of child-rearing. Now I began to hunt on the printed page for my answers. I read through two shelves in the public library, everything from the most watered-down version of Freud to professional texts, which I scarcely understood.

But what I read, in spite of differing vocabularies and differing emphases, all boiled down to the same thing. The troubled child comes from the troubled family. Trouble begins with a disturbed mother. For one reason or another she consciously or unconsciously rejects the child. Since she does not know how to love, she cannot teach him how to love. Therefore he lives, in his turn, unable to develop meaningful relationships with other human beings. The illness spreads to the family. Sometimes the family uses the "sick" member as a scapegoat, a focus for all its own frustrations, and the family really wills this member not to get well, because they need him as he is.

Well, let us begin, I thought, with me, the mother. Was she troubled or disturbed? Now, at this point, she was. Now definitely I did not have the joy and energy one ought to have for one's children. Surely Tony needed all the strength I could summon to help him through his bad time. The other three, in their different ways, needed me not only for normal reasons but also for special reassurance, considering what Tony was doing to their lives. I was wanted in so many different directions! And I was drifting, tired, making an effort in everything I did. I didn't feel like hearing Sarah's piano or going downtown to buy shoes with her and Jane. I didn't feel like spending an afternoon in school at Freddy's swimming meet. I went, I put on a happy face, but my heart was not in it.

Maybe I had always been like this? And concealed it even from myself? Maybe I wasn't the real mother I had thought I was? Acting, perhaps? Playing a part? These books all said that the mothers of emotionally disturbed children were "cold women," self-absorbed, unable to give. Was I a cold woman? How did you know what you were? I had no basis for comparison with anyone else.

And what of Jack? A man must be a strong, masculine father, calm and firm in authority, so that his son would know from observing him what it was to be a man. He had to be patient, consistent, vigorous, and, although it did not say so exactly, one got the impression that the best father was athletic.

Jack was fairly unathletic. He liked a game of tennis now and then, as much for the fresh air and relaxation at the club as for the game itself. His favorite outdoor activities were bird-watching and, of course, photography. In my opinion, Jack was firm, fair and kind. Certainly he was masculine; certainly he was head of the family. But he was also inconsistent as far as Tony was concerned, because he had no more idea than I of what to do when Tony spat in Sarah's plate, say. Sometimes he ordered him to leave the table. Sometimes he sat down and talked and tried to find out why Tony felt so upset. Sometimes he took away Tony's allowance for a week. But more often lately after he had been up since six o'clock in the morning and had seen thirty patients during the day, he was just plain furious and walloped Tony. And afterward sat contritely in our room talking things over, wondering what we were going to do.

Was it Jack's fault? Should he have had some

inborn male instinct that would know how to handle a son? Everything that I read seemed to indicate that a mature man can easily rear a healthy son in his own image. Whose fault was this, then?

There came a morning when Tony refused to go to school. He had stayed home the previous day, pleading a sore throat, and since Jack had already left for the hospital I had had no way of checking his throat. On the second morning, however, Jack was still home. He looked at the boy's throat, saw there was nothing wrong and told him to go to school.

"I won't go," said Tony. "And you can't make me."

I called Dr. Maxwell and asked him what to do. Surely this was an issue that required a specific answer.

"I cannot discuss it with you," he said. He was quite cool. "As a matter of fact, I do not want to talk to you any more on the telephone without Tony's permission."

I replaced the telephone with a feeling of humiliation and anger, like a chastised child myself. It made no sense at all to me. The relation between therapist and patient must remain confidential, I understood that; but in a situation involving a child so young this elaborate hands-off attitude seemed unrealistic. Particularly since we had to live with Tony and handle situations at once as they arose.

I felt that Dr. Maxwell and Tony were in league against me, that I was the enemy, rather than the mother who would have given anything in the world to help her son.

Tony solved the problem. "I will go back to school if I don't have to see Doctor Maxwell again," he told me.

"But why? He seemed so nice." I floundered. "He does want to help you and—"

"He doesn't help me," Tony insisted.

I found myself in the odd position of defending Dr. Maxwell. "But you have to give him time!"

"I said I'm not going to go any more and I'm going to tell him so."

Jack went along for the next appointment. He and I waited while Tony went into the doctor. After only fifteen minutes, Tony emerged and walked straight out to the car. The doctor spoke to us.

"I'm not going to see Tony any more. He does not want to come and actually he may well be correct. We do not seem to have established any relationship. He has not been willing to talk to me or to go beyond playing chess."

Twice a week for a whole year and all they had been doing was playing chess?

"Perhaps you ought to take him to someone else," Dr. Maxwell said.

That was honest enough, but why had he taken a whole year to come to that conclusion? "Or perhaps he will want to return to me of his own volition. At any rate, he cannot be forced to come here. Before you leave," he said, addressing Jack, "I should like to speak to you alone for a moment."

What terrible thing did he want to tell Jack

out of my presence? Something awful about Tony
that perhaps he wanted to spare me? I waited,
cold with fear, until, after a short while, Jack
came out. We walked down the street toward our
car.

"What is it?" I asked.

"He thinks I ought to see a psychiatrist."

"You? Not me?"

"Just me."

"But why?"

"He says that today when Tony told him that
he wasn't coming any more, he detected something in Tony's remarks—he didn't tell me what—
that suggested a poor relationship with me. He
thinks maybe I need some help."

"How ridiculous!" I cried. "There's nothing the
matter with you!"

"He didn't mean it as an insult," Jack said. "If
it is necessary, I will go."

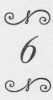

6

NOW Jack and I were almost frantic; we had to find a doctor who could do something. Jack asked everyone who was in a position to give advice. We wanted the most competent psychiatrist, a man who was experienced with adolescents; we did not care what he charged. If he should see fit to put either one or both of us in treatment with Tony, we were ready to do that too.

And so we came to Dr. Alden Collins. It took some persuasion before Tony would agree to go to another doctor. But at that time we still had hours during which Tony and I were able to achieve a little understanding. I thought that Tony really knew something was very wrong and growing worse, that he was frightened and wanted to be helped, although he could not possibly have admitted it.

But we were concerned that, once having consented to go, Tony would waste the time as he had done with Dr. Maxwell. "That won't happen," Dr. Collins assured us firmly. "I don't permit that."

Here was a welcome change indeed. And another difference was that this doctor did not treat us, the parents, like interlopers; he knew we had come to him freely because we wanted advice and did not have the answers within ourselves. He had a direct manner; he was sympathetic without being maudlin; we felt that he understood our fears and uncertainties. Above all, he was hopeful.

"There's no doubt that Tony was born with a defective personality," he explained. "Why or how these things happen, we simply don't know. But you cannot blame yourself or your husband too much. It is not constructive to look backward. Only forward. That's common sense."

"But if he was born with a defective personality, how can he be helped?"

"By teaching him to live with his handicap. By re-education. Primarily of him, and then, to some extent, of you and your husband, so that you will understand how to help him to help himself."

"Doctor, I see what you mean about not looking backward. Yet it would relieve me greatly if you would give me some general idea of what we have done wrong."

"It's not always things that you actually did 'wrong.' It's things that life did, circumstances that very often couldn't have been helped or changed. For instance, the prenatal influence. Your undoubted tension and distress over your husband's being overseas when the baby was born. Then at two, a particularly sensitive age, you left him when your father died, and then a few weeks later left him to have your seond baby. Leaving a child of that age is a kind of abandonment, terrifying to him. Then, of course, you moved quite a lot, three times during his lifetime, and that's very unsettling for a child who is insecure to begin with. However, I don't feel really disturbed about Tony. Working together, with effort and patience, I believe we will make great progress."

One day I told Dr. Collins what Jack had said about Tony's having schizophrenia.

"He thinks that?" the doctor repeated with some surprise.

"Well, I don't know whether he still does, whether he's really made up his mind. After all, he isn't a psychiatrist and he acknowledges his own limitations, but I think the fear must still lurk in his mind."

"Well, that's too bad," the doctor said. "I'd be glad to have him come in and talk to me about it. There's no reason for him to be living with a fear like that. It's quite unfounded, really. I would characterize Tony as schizoid," he said carefully, "which is not the same at all, you know. Many overly quiet, timid, insecure children have schizoid tendencies, which means that, untreated in psychotherapy, they *may* develop schizophrenia. It's a kind of warning; look at it that way. A warning to take preventive measures. But even so, these children usually do *not* develop schizophrenia and we are certainly taking every step to assure that Tony will not."

"Then you really do have hope for Tony!"

"Indeed, I have," Dr. Collins answered firmly.

"I can't wait to tell Jack!" I cried. "Only I do wish he weren't such a pessimist."

"Well, it's good to face reality, but in this case, really, tell your husband that while your boy is troubled indeed, he's not as sick as he may think. Tell him I said so. He must try to have positive feelings within himself about Tony. They will be communicated to the whole family, especially to Tony. Above all, your husband must not let Tony think that he believes he is sick. The boy must feel hopeful about himself. He must feel we know he is capable of doing better and that he will do better."

"Doctor," I said, feeling for the first time that I would ask all the questions I had in mind, "I know that in these cases you cannot have an exact time-table, but have you any thoughts about how long it may take for some real change to take place?"

He considered a moment. "Seventeen will see a turning point. If Tony is not over these problems at the age of seventeen, then he will not get over them. But," he added, "I believe as firmly as one can, without making promises, that he *will* be over them by then. I wouldn't be working with him if I didn't think I could bring him through with success. His own intelligence will help a great deal, you know."

"In other words, either he will return to normal or have to go"—my mouth did not want to form the words—"to a mental hospital" (the terror, the panic: the snake pit).

"Normal? Whatever that is. Still, I understand what you mean. Oh, I don't ever see Tony as a big man on campus, an extrovert, a bond salesman. He isn't made that way; you know that. But I can see him," Dr. Collins said thoughtfully, "as a scholar, doing some kind of quiet research, in which he will be pretty much alone, not dependent upon making an impression on other people. I can see a successful life for him. The world needs people like him, and I believe we can bring him to that point."

These were words to lift the heart. A far cry from the cold silences of Dr. Maxwell.

I thought of something else. "Suppose he stays the same, neither better nor worse? Not needing to be hospitalized but not well either? Just the way he is now?"

"It doesn't work that way," Dr. Collins assured me. "Change is axiomatic in human affairs, you know; nothing stays the same. Things either get worse or they get better."

On the way home I remember I turned on the car radio and sang like a young girl. I felt a surge of energy and confidence. I could, I would, manage anything. You could surmount any obstacle; keep up your courage and nothing in the world can beat you!

I tried to get some of this feeling across to Jack. I pleaded and sometimes scolded. "Tony isn't as sick as you think he is. Why won't you be more hopeful? Why don't you believe Doctor Collins? You'd be the first to be exasperated if a patient tried to tell you how to operate on him. Well, you're just as ignorant in this field. Why won't you admit that Doctor Collins knows more about Tony's problems than you do?"

"You don't have to know much to know more

than I do," Jack would answer. "But I suppose," he said, sighing, "I'll have to trust in him. And trust in luck."

Sometimes, though, in another mood, he would say, "You're right. One has to have faith. I wish I could be more like you. I don't know what I would do without you."

And I would feel, I must admit, so virtuous and sensible, and just a little smug about my own fortitude and good cheer.

After several months of association with Dr. Collins, he informed us that neither Jack nor I was in need of psychiatric treatment. What we did need badly was reeducation in the treatment of Tony, who surely required more skillful understanding than we had been giving him.

"From my observation of you and my picture of home which I get from Tony, I must say that I don't see grave faults in either of you. You are quite unsure of yourselves, rather afraid of Tony, and I think you are quite tense. But then, under the circumstances, that's understandable."

The soundproofing in Dr. Collins' office was not the best, so there were a few times when, sitting in the silent waiting room, I could not help but hear some phrases of the dialogue taking place inside.

"You're not as beset with troubles as you think you are," the doctor chided Tony. "You told me yourself that your parents aren't so bad, that in fact they're pretty good to you—"

"Yes," I heard Tony interrupt. "I know they love me. My mother says I am really a wonderful person underneath all the awful things that I do."

"Tell me, Tony, what do your brother and sisters say when you do such nasty things?"

"They think I ought to love Daddy and Mommy. They think Daddy and Mommy are nice to us."

"Well now, maybe you ought to think about that some more. The next time you feel angry, remember that and try to do something constructive with your anger instead of letting it out on people who are trying to help you. Go home tonight and see how well you can do."

Remarkably, some of this attitude rubbed off on Tony, because during that first year, after almost every visit to Dr. Collins he used to be in a better mood, briefly. Visits were made after school and usually Tony's good spirits lasted for the rest of the afternoon and through dinner, so that on that one evening in the week we were able to look forward to some peace and order.

Jack always tried to take advantage of those evenings by offering Tony his sole attention, as if by feeding these responsive moments he might be able to get hold of his son and keep hold.

But the hold never lasted. They would go into the den to have a game of checkers. I would leave the room, remembering the importance of nurturing a sound male relationship between son and father. For a short while I would hear the normal murmur of voices. Then rising anger, Jack's firm remonstrance, Tony's rage and a crash. That was Tony, either losing the game, which he could not bear to do, or perhaps just displeased with the way his father played. So he had simply hurled the checker board to the floor and very often the table along with it.

It was the pattern to which we had gradually become accustomed, except that now, in a thirteen-year-old, such violent, childish anger was deeply shocking.

We handled this with the same inconsistency, according to mood and degree of fatigue, I am afraid. Most of the time Jack made a valiant effort to be patient. I used to hear him talking quietly to Tony, explaining why certain behavior elicits certain responses from others. "You get what you give," I heard him say. Then he used to ask Tony to confide in him, so that he might help him, rather than just vent his feelings.

Sometimes, though, I heard the sound of a smart slap. Then I knew Jack had come to the end of his endurance, and I felt sharp pity for them both, father and son.

There were times during those years when Tony seemed to turn to me for comfort. In oblique ways he would briefly reveal what was going on inside.

Once, for instance, he called me into his room to ask my advice about one of his classmates.

His name was Andy White, and Tony felt sorry for him. "Nobody likes him. He has no friends and he's really a nice boy. Why is that?"

I asked Tony to tell me about him.

"Well, you know, sometimes he stands around during lunch hour with the boys and they all tell jokes. But when Andy tells a joke, nobody laughs. Of course, he doesn't know how to tell a joke very well. And he walks through the hall between classes all alone. I wish I could help him."

I wished he could, too. And I tried to explain that there just are some lucky and unlucky accidents of personality. Some people simply lacked the sparkle to attract others even though they were perfectly nice. They had a certain shyness which made it hard to get started.

Then was there nothing to be done about it? Tony asked.

"Well," I suggested, "maybe this boy ought to look around for some other quiet boy like himself. In a big school like yours there must be some other boys who haven't yet made a lot of friends. If he found one of them and invited him home, he could make at least one friend. He wouldn't feel so lonely. And when the others saw that, they'd want to get to know him too, and gradually he could make a group around himself."

"But why don't people like him in the first place?"

I was so helpless. And I thought: Children, people are so cruel. Why, when they must see his need for just a few words, do they withhold them?

So the pattern of Tony's life did not really change. He went to school and did his work superlatively; he behaved well there, indeed, too well. His moral standards allowed not the smallest infringement of the smallest rule. Every afternoon he came home alone, unbefriended. Every night he created chaos in the house.

He made taunting Jane a ritual at the dinner table. He taunted her about her freckles, her skinny height, her big feet. She tried to take it as a joke. I used to wink at her and shake my head but, after all, she was only a child and after a certain amount of jeering, tears began to fall. Jack would order Tony to stop, which he refused to do. Then he would order him to leave the table, with similar results. Naturally, for the sake of family dignity and his own discipline, Jack could not allow him to get away with that. He would threaten to remove him bodily.

"Try to catch me!" Tony would fling a challenge. And on rare occasions of extreme exasperation, Jack would light out after the boy. Round and round the table they would race until Tony would make his escape to the yard through the back door. It was a pitiable and disgraceful sight; Jack, forty years old, would be left short of breath and red in the face from exertion and defeat.

In private, when Tony was calm, I used to remonstrate with him. "For your own sake, don't start these things. If you don't care about your sister's feelings, think of your own. Do you enjoy making a mess out of your own dinner? Think how good it would feel for you and for all of us to eat a peaceful meal for a change."

He was contrite. "I'm sorry, Ma, I'll remember, I'm through doing that."

But the next day, or an hour later, he did it again. He never learned, never seemed capable of learning from experience.

I discussed this with Dr. Collins in private consultation.

"You see," he said, in friendly admonition, "it comes back to your own personality and your husband's. You have both really abdicated your authority for so long that it is hard to reinstate it. Go home and use force! Stand up to the boy!"

"When he picks up a vase and throws it?"

"Pick up another and throw it back! Lose your temper! Show him that he cannot get away with that sort of thing. That you just will not stand for it. This is your will against his."

"What a dreadful way to live!" I protested. "Who can live that way?"

"Who can live the way you're living now?" He continued: "If your husband cannot enforce orders then you will have to."

"I wish Jack were home more. I wish he were a Scoutmaster-type who would know how to control a boy."

"Well, he isn't, and you can't change him. Yet many women raise their sons without a husband at all. Widows rear sons competently. But it doesn't always go easily. Assert yourself. You can, you know."

There was something so encouraging in this good will and optimism. "I'll try," I responded. "And I'll stop being afraid."

Dr. Collins smiled. "Good. You'll develop more confidence after you have handled just one situation with some success."

I had barely stopped the car in the garage when I heard the turmoil in the house: frenzied barking of the dogs, shrieks that sounded like Jane's. I raced in through the back door, and there was Hanna pinning Jane's arms back so she could not get at Tony, who stood grinning with fists up like a boxer's.

"Do something to him. Kill him!" Jane

screamed at me. Her face was dirty with tears and her stamping feet came down hard on my toe.

"Mrs. Wilson," Hanna cried, "you just ought to see what this boy's done to Jane's room. It's a shame, I tell you. This boy ain't fit to live with. I'd put him out of this house if he was mine. He ain't good for nothing."

"Go to hell, you fat slob," Tony said.

"Hit him, Mommy. You never do anything!" Jane shrieked.

I tried to make myself heard above the bedlam. "What happened?"

"Go upstairs and look!"

I flew upstairs. Freddy and Sarah were on the floor of Jane's room trying to sort out a pile of books which had been swept from the shelves. Crayons, paint, all the contents of the bureau drawers, were strewn all over the charming white and yellow room. I stood there, sick at the ugly destruction, at the sight of Jane's Christmas doll, her treasure of curls and lace, flung on the pile with one arm broken off.

"Tony did it all," Sarah cried. "He did all this, Mommy; he's a bad boy. I hate him."

"I wish he would die," Freddy said. "Why don't you put him in the garbage?"

Heaven help me, I could have done so, willingly, at that moment. All the calm resolve that had filled me half an hour ago in the doctor's office simply ebbed away. I wanted to sit down and cry. I wanted to walk out of the house and not come back. I wanted to beat Tony, just beat him until I felt relief.

But I took a deep breath and went downstairs.

Tony was not there. In the kitchen Jane was sobbing quietly on Hanna's arm. I walked over and laid my hand on the pathetic little head.

"Jane, darling, I'll fix everything. Oh, I'm so sorry. I'll fix your room; I'll get you another doll. I won't ever let it happen again—"

"Yes you will," Jane said. "You and Daddy can't do anything; you're afraid of Tony."

How explain to a child? "Jane, dear, we are trying so hard. I know you can't understand, but Tony is upset and we are trying to help him. I really promise that I won't ever let him do anything like this again. Hanna," I asked, "how did it happen?"

"Well, I can't be watching things every minute, you know; that boy's—"

"I know you can't," I said quickly. "Of course not."

"I was in the basement taking the clothes out of the washing machine and I heard this screaming and yelling. I came up and found Tony fighting with the girls and Freddy. He was hitting and almost killed them. Then he ran upstairs away from me— There he goes now running across the yard. You, Tony. You come in here, you devil!"

"I'll handle him," I said. I went outside and confronted Tony just as he was about to slip out at the gate.

"Tony," I said sternly, "I'm going to get at the bottom of this. We have all had more than we can stand—"

A gob of spit struck me full in the face.

You must get down to his level, the doctor had

said. *Give exactly what you get*. I spat back, full
in Tony's face.

For an instant he looked at me in astonishment. "You'll learn," he said. "I do whatever I
want to do and no one stops me." He gave me a
ringing slap on the cheek, and before I could
recover from the shock and pain, he had opened
the gate and was gone down the street.

I stood there stunned. This could not possibly
be the right way. I felt dirty and ashamed. How
could I keep the respect of my other children, to
say nothing of my own?

The next day I tried another tack. Tony was in
the kitchen having bread and jam. I talked quickly
before he could get away.

"I want to tell you something," I said. "I love
you, but I hate the way you act. I want to help
you act better so you will be happier. Will you let
me help you? May we start again?"

In essence I must have told him this some hundreds of times during our years of trouble. I don't
know what sort of answer I expected. There was
none. He retreated hastily from the kitchen, but
not before I was able to see that his eyes were full
of tears.

Who is he, my son? What is he? Out of the
multiplicity of events, through the chaotic days, I
remember this persistent strand of thought: is he
a timid child to be strengthened or a bully to be
kept in hand? One person in the house, another
person outside? With a flash of astonished insight
it came to me that Tony *was* two people. Two
people! For it came to me too that he was no
different now than he had been when he was three

years old and could not defend his own pail and shovel in the sandbox, but would go inside and knock his baby sister to the floor. No different at all, only older and bigger.

In spite of all my effort, my confidence in the good Dr. Collins gradually began to ebb away.

In the doctor's waiting room I used to see a woman whose son had the appointment just after Tony's. Sometimes she would come alone to see the doctor, and occasionally when there was no one else in the waiting room we talked to each other. I never asked her name nor did she ask mine, but we spoke freely with an understanding that neither of us ever could have with any other woman. She told me that her boy had been coming to Dr. Collins for the past nine years. "I don't know what I would do without him," she said. "He's been wonderfully kind. Especially now that Warren won't go to school. We have a tutor. My husband is away a good deal and the only peace I have is when the tutor is in the house. When Warren and I are alone I am beside myself. Tell me, have you got any other children besides this boy?"

I told her we had three others.

"You're so fortunate," she said wistfully. "We only have Warren. He was such a problem by the time he was three that I just didn't want to try again. I'm sorry now. And how are your other children?"

"They're fine," I said, understanding what she meant. "Thank God, they are all fine."

"Then you have something to live for. My husband and I often think— You know," she interrupted herself in a rush of confidence, "although I still think the world of Doctor Collins I don't believe in him any more. Because after all these years Warren is no better. We've lost him. We have no son. Sometimes I can't help thinking it would have been kinder never to have had a son at all! Someday I shall be left alone with Warren—my husband is not well—and I'm afraid."

She was not speaking so much of her personal safety, I knew, but of the long stretch of years ahead.

"Oh well," she finished with false cheer, "we have to keep trying, don't we?"

My mind kept returning to her; she seemed to be a reasonable person, not overly emotional about her trouble. Nine years, she had said, with no change. I tried not to think about it. Besides, each case is different, isn't it?

Certainly I would not have changed places for a minute with this woman whose only child was an emotional wreck. But I had to admit that her life was less complex than ours. We were rearing two families. There was one set of rules for Tony, and another for Jane, Sarah and Freddy. The three were required to wash their hands before dinner, to sit up straight at the table, to speak respectfully. Tony slouched and spilled and thrust his dirty hands into the mashed potatoes but no one said anything about it. We were thankful, we thought the evening a success if only he kept the peace and left everyone alone. This standard made sense for Tony; first things first, and the first thing was to put him at ease and never mind the dirt. But making that clear to the other children was difficult indeed. All they could see was the unfairness.

Of all the tumultuous, troubled hours of our days, the dinner hour was the worst. All our tensions seemed to reach their peak around the table. The good food was swallowed without being tasted; the bowl of roses in the center a mockery. I can see us all now: Jack at the head, determinedly trying to guide his family into some kind of cheerful, neutral conversation; me, silently spurring everyone on to eat faster, to get the meal over with before Tony could provoke chaos.

As I look back, I think how remarkable it was that the three younger children understood as much as they did. Yet I realize that, in spite of all the trouble, they were certain of our love for them. And so they were able to accept the situation and to live with it in spite of its seeming injustice.

There were changes in their routine, however: they stopped bringing friends home. Our house, which had been open house for everyone, was so no longer. More and more often Jane and the twins began to go elsewhere after school; they never invited anyone any more.

Nor, come to think of it, did Jack and I. Time drifts imperceptibly when you are preoccupied, and some months passed before I became aware we no longer saw our friends. We lived in dread that someone might come unannounced into the middle of a scene.

We rarely went out. Hanna told us that she simply could not manage Tony by herself, and obviously no one else could. I was in dread that the turmoil might soon come to be too much for her and she might leave. What would I do then? Hanna was old but strong; she had some control over Tony when he was in a tantrum. Alone I would be able to do nothing. I was not afraid that Tony wanted to hurt anyone; indeed, I was certain he would never intend to do so. But in a free-for-all, especially with a boy as strong as he, anything can happen accidentally.

The doctor was still hopeful and unperturbed by my reports. "What you have here is a battle of the wills. Tony has had the upper hand for so long in your household that you cannot hope to change things overnight. But he will learn. With the proper handling on your part, I assure you he will learn."

I repeated this to Jack, who answered, "In other words, if we explain emphatically and often enough that we will not tolerate the things he does, he will finally stop doing them?"

"Something like that."

My husband spoke a short, vulgar word. "You think Tony's a bad boy? That's all he is, a bad boy?"

"You know I don't mean that. He's undisciplined. He needs to get into the habit of proper behavior. It's a kind of reflex process, Doctor Collins says. A kind of habituation."

"Louise, I tell you this is all poppycock. Tony cannot help what he does. He has no control over it."

"That's not what the doctor says."

"Then he and I part company, psychiatrist or no."

Strange, how the tables had turned! Not so long before, it had been I who thought he had "problems," that he needed "help," and Jack who thought it was simply a case of an overindulgent mother. Now it was he who thought the situation more crucial, more ominous than I did.

"Jack, we have to try," I sighed. "Even if you don't agree with Doctor Collins, what else is there for us to do?"

"I know. I suppose it's not fair of me to weaken your hope and faith. I only wish I had more faith in the whole business myself. Or that I knew of something better."

Doggedly we went through each relentless day. About midsummer Dr. Collins himself proposed we try tranquilizers on Tony. The boy flew into a rage at the suggestion. He denied he had any need of tranquilizers or any other help. The doctor suggested we put them secretly into his milk. The only trouble with that was we never had any way of knowing how much milk he would drink. Sometimes he did not drink enough to matter and other times he drank so much that he slept half the day.

We drifted. In spite of all my optimistic exhortations to myself and to Jack, I felt it undeniably—we were spinning faster and faster downstream.

Violence became more frequent and more painful. I remember Jane's first supper party. We had bought her a lemon-yellow dress: how can I ever forget that dress? She was waiting at the front door for her date when suddenly Tony ran out of the kitchen, his upraised hand smeared with jelly. Too late, I saw him coming and rushed to head him off, but not before he had left a wide grape-colored smear across Jane's shoulder.

Utter chaos: Jane's piteous scream, Tony's fit of evil laughter as he raced round and round the room, with me running uselessly behind.

Hanna came from the kitchen with a wet cloth and began to dab at the stain. And I lost my head. I was close to frenzy at that moment. I remember exactly what I said, for it tormented me long afterward.

"You monster!" I shrieked at Tony. "I hate the sight of you! Why don't you run out and throw yourself in the river? Why don't you do yourself and all of us a favor? Why don't you get out of our lives?"

Into this scene came my husband, after a long day's work.

"Daddy!" Jane cried hysterically. "Daddy, look what Tony did to me!"

Out on the street a horn blew. Hanna gave the people some excuse, I don't know what. Tony escaped to his room, locking the door behind him.

"You'd better not come out, you devil!" Jack cried, losing his own temper after all the good resolutions and all the insight. "I'll beat you to a pulp if you do!"

Jane had thrown herself on the sofa. I tried to take her in my arms, but she was all flying feet and flailing arms. She was beside herself.

"I wish I could die!" she screamed. "I can't stand this house! I can't stand it!"

These were no ordinary tears, this was no usual grief to be reasoned and gently talked away by a loving mother. This was hysteria—the same hysteria I now felt rush through me.

Jack must have seen it too. He had quickly taken command of himself, as always, and now led me to the porch. "Sit down, Louise. Take a deep breath and keep calm. We'll get through this."

Mutely, gratefully, I obeyed. There was no dinner. Hanna removed the food. I heard Jack's firm "professional" voice, heard Jane's cries, after a long time, die away. Then I heard him going upstairs with her.

I sat there, hearing the small sounds of my stricken family. Jack came downstairs again and got a dish of ice cream for Jane. Still I sat there, thinking of nothing, just gone blank.

"Don't you want a little something to eat?" Hanna asked. When I shook my head, she said: "I don't know what you're all going to do. I'm sure I don't. One thing, that doctor there, he sure don't know what he's doing!"

My own confidence in the hopeful Dr. Collins had just about vanished. And my conscience hurt. After the concern over Jane and the bloom of her summer evening so brutally destroyed, had come thoughts about Tony. I saw suddenly, in spite of Dr. Collins, that all this *was* beyond the boy's control and not his fault. And I, I his mother, had told him to go out and die. And the worst thing was that I had meant it when I said it. And Tony must know that I had meant it.

I told the doctor about it next time I saw him.

"Don't feel bad about it," he said. "As a matter of fact, it may have done Tony some good to hear you talk that way. It may bring him to reality to know that other people have feelings, that other people, not only he, can get angry and say horrible things."

"But I am so worried over Jane and my twins," I said. "What kind of a life are we giving them? Why should they grow up like his? It's corrupting, his filthy language, his savage temper . . ."

"A great many people have to grow up under worse handicaps, you know that. Go down into any slum and look."

"But will it damage them?"

"The healthy human being can stand a very great deal. The sick collapse under slight pressures, but the well can bear much more than you realize."

Still, it did not seem right to expect them to bear it just because it was possible for them to do so. And I said so.

"I have other families who have put up with this sort of thing much longer than you have. I have one family who have had a boy like Tony for seven years. And they do not complain, at least to me."

"They live the way we live?"

"They do." Dr. Collins spoke rather grimly.

It seemed to me that he was trying to make me feel ashamed of my weakness. I wanted to ask how long you were supposed to live this way. If after seven years, those people were still putting up with it, what was the time limit? Were you just supposed to go on forever?

Night after night now Jack and I went without sleep. Tony was never tired; he could be awake, it seemed, for twenty hours. He used to sit in our bedroom reading in the wing chair beside the fireplace and he would not be dislodged. No order, no plea, no appeal to reason or even to mercy when we were desperate for sleep were of any avail. After a while we discovered that sometimes if we said nothing, if we got into bed and lay there quietly taking no notice of him, he would depart of his own volition. But it had to be of his own volition. He simply could not take orders no matter how decently and courteously given.

Sometimes he left us alone at bedtime but developed a habit of coming into our room at three o'clock in the morning, switching on the bright lights so that we were startled awake in fright.

"I can't sleep; why should you?" he would demand. Then would come the fireside vigil, lasting into the early morning hours, and Jack had to get up to operate at six-thirty.

So many things come back to me from that year. You would be surprised at the things well-meaning people can do to you in your time of greatest desperation.

I recall the wife of the one friend who knew our situation and who had always been most sympathetic. "You had better do something about Tony soon, Louise. I must tell you for your own good. Jack's a wonderful man, a good man, but . . . well, it wouldn't be hard for him to find a woman with a quiet little apartment, a good dinner, some peace after his long day. Instead of coming home to a nerve-racking mess like this! You'd better do something before he reaches the end of his endurance."

Hanna warned, "You'd better keep an eye on your husband; he looks bad. He ain't going to last long working the way he does and can't have his dinner or a night's rest in peace. Why, only last Monday I see where Doctor Shore dropped dead and he was only forty-nine years old."

That fear at least was very real to me. I remarked to Dr. Collins one day that Jack looked ill. "And I am terribly afraid that he might have a heart attack from all the strain."

The doctor nodded. "It's entirely possible. You must be prepared to face it."

"But how? If anything happens to him, how will I manage with Tony? The two of us together can barely do it now."

Dr. Collins did not answer me. Then out of terror came a wave of foreknowledge. I would just have to manage. I would not have any choice.

I had never been particularly observant of religious creed. But I think I had always been, and I know I am now, religious in the deepest sense. I understand how small I am, how incapable of understanding the nature of God, how little I know of who I am or where I am going. I only know that I must do my best and have faith in the greater power and accept. I lay awake that night while Jack was out on an emergency call, thinking long thoughts.

Suddenly I heard strange sounds in Tony's room. I hurried out of bed and went in.

He was standing with his head pressed against

the wall and crying. I came up and put my hands on him.

He turned and laid his head on my shoulder, then put his arms around me. "Ma, I want to tell you something. You and Dad, you are the best parents a boy ever had. And I make you so miserable."

I felt his wet face on my shoulder; my own eyes were wet.

"I love you so," he said, "you and Dad. I want to live happily with you."

"Tony, dear, we love you so much too. And as long as we remember that, nothing else is really important, things will turn out fine. You'll see."

He raised his head, his marvelous eyes, so trusting, so clear, "Will they, Ma? You really believe they will?"

"I know it, Tony." I remember the exact spot where we were standing, beside the desk at the window with the snow-covered branch cutting across the pane. "I know they will, Tony."

"YOU GOD-DAMN SON OF A BITCH! GET THE HELL OUT OF MY ROOM BEFORE I KILL YOU!"

I got out. I fled across the hall into my own room and locked the door. For a long time I sat there in the dark, trembling before something terrible and unknown.

Jack said, "He should be hospitalized. I don't give a hoot what any doctor tells me about 'emotional maladjustment.' The boy is terribly sick and ought to be in the hospital."

Dr. Collins would not hear of it. "No," he said,

"you misread the symptoms. Tony looks and sounds a great deal worse than he is. Don't let these words of his frighten the wits out of you."

He wanted to give Tony every chance. Right or wrong, that was his motive. For that I was and am still grateful to him.

Yet in spite of my gratitude I began to feel that he was somewhat less understanding than when we had gone to him two years before. I tried to make him see that Tony was growing worse, harder to live with.

"He follows me around the house literally every instant," I said. "He doesn't let me out of his sight from the moment I enter the house."

"Why should that surprise you? You know he has an Oedipal attachment."

"Yes, but now he follows me to spit and curse at me. I cannot get along with him at all, whereas until recently I used to be able to reach him *sometimes*. And he does such queer things, like going out in February, in New England, in cotton shirt sleeves without a coat!"

"Has he caught cold?"

"No, strangely enough, he han't."

"Well, why worry about it? When he feels the need, he'll put some warm clothes on." Dr. Collins paused. "You know, I've been thinking, maybe you ought to put Tony into a boarding school."

"What boarding school?"

"There are schools for boys with emotional problems, where they get psychiatric supervision along with a standard education. It would give Tony the structured environment, the order and authority that he lacks in your house, since apparently neither you nor your husband can gain authority over him."

No, and you couldn't either, I thought. And I asked, "You really think that would be best?"

"The best would be to keep him at home as long as you can, but if you cannot do it, then I would say that this would be next best."

"Where shall I find such a school?"

"I'll send you a list of possibilities. Then there are always advertisements in the school sections of the newspaper. Go look them over and then we'll discuss it."

Suddenly everything came to a head. One afternoon Tony came in and announced he was through with Dr. Collins.

"What do you mean?" I cried. "You like him so much and—"

"He's a jerk. They're all a lot of jerks. I sit at the desk and give him a snow job and he sits on the other side of the desk and gives me a snow job. I'm not going to do it any more."

"Tony, please, no matter what you think, please listen to me! Listen to your father! After all, he's a doctor and he knows what's best for you. You'll have to admit that, won't you?"

"I said I'm not going any more and I won't and nobody can make me."

And nobody could make him. He knew it. We knew it. In spite of my waning confidence in Dr. Collins, he had nevertheless been a support. Now he was gone and we stood wavering. We were absolutely alone.

7

I HAD never known that the great metropolitan dailies are filled with advertisements for special schools. Of course, they all sound equally attractive and competent. I began to pore over them. I called several on the telephone and had to rule out the first few because they would not even consider taking a child who would not come willingly. But that was at the core of our problem: Tony was absolutely unwilling to leave home.

We visited several of the schools and were very discouraged. To begin with, the physical environments were shocking. Some of these places were so poor and barren they would make a normal person feel depressed.

I remember one which sounded most promising when I talked to the director on the telephone. He was a well-spoken man with a doctorate and was a specialist in the psychology of the emotionally disturbed adolescent. His school occupied a piece of acreage carved out of second-growth woods and sumac scrub on a main highway. He and his wife lived in a small frame house, and about fifty feet away were the students' quarters, in a long frame building shaped like a railway car. It was divided into cubicles much like a boarding kennel, clean, well-heated and bare.

Outside there was a basketball net nailed to a tree and a very small pond "where they can skate when it freezes over," we were told.

"What else is there for recreation?" we asked.

"Oh, we take nature walks, we drive into town."

The town through which we had passed consisted of four or five blocks of stores and a shabby movie theater. I couldn't imagine what the boys could do after they got there.

"We have a psychiatrist who comes over on Thursdays," the director said "And of course the curriculum is college preparatory. I teach and I have a well-qualified assistant. We have some very fine students here."

"And the fee?" Jack inquired. He was merely filling the silence, because I knew he never would have left Tony here. I wondered what kind of parents possibly could have done so.

"Five hundred dollars a month," was the reply. "All inclusive."

Jack said we would think it over and have Tony's doctor get in touch with him.

"I do want to add one thing," the man said. "Whether or not you decide to send your son to my school, I must advise you to send him somewhere. Don't try to keep him at home."

He was really very decent; undoubtedly, given funds, he could have set up something much better. He was surely aware of how disgracefully inadequate his facilities were. But it only showed how desperate the need is and that people in desperate need settle for almost anything.

"You can see for yourselves that your boy isn't improving at home. If anything, he is getting worse, as the family's endurance wears thin."

"That's true."

"And it is simply not fair to the other children. Take the boy away before irreparable damage is done. That's my most candid advice to you."

We thanked him and drove away. His admonitions made a great deal more sense to me than what I had been hearing from Dr. Collins about endurance.

Or did it only make more sense because it offered me an easy way out, because it was what I wanted to be told?

Now events picked up momentum. What had been a very gradual descent, with interludes of apparently slight improvement, now suddenly became that steep-pitched slide. The gentle springtime was ominous. There was no Dr. Collins to run to via the telephone in emergencies. So often his advice had been useless or impossible to carry out; still it had been something, a willing ear, an encouraging word. Now Jack and I alone, or rather Hanna and I during the day, had to hold the fort. And fort it was, an armed encampment.

Tony would come home from school and sit in front of the television. For the first time his work fell off; his interim report card was the first poor one in a lifetime of A's. But instead of studying, he sat in front of the television, brooding rather than seeing.

No one dared come into the room. When one of

the other children ventured in, there would be a shout of rage: *Get the hell out of here!* And they got out, because there was nothing I could do except to beg them to keep away from Tony. And they knew there was nothing I could do.

He no longer came to the table to eat with the family. He waited until we were all finished and then helped himself in the refrigerator. He refused to touch any food that I had prepared or handled; even a bakery cake, if my hand had untied the string. Not until years later did we hear he was afraid his food was being poisoned.

We were floundering. I found myself, in my desperation, quarreling with Jack.

"Will you find a place for him, get him out of this house? What kind of a father can watch his family die by inches like this? You're a doctor. Can't you do something, anything?"

It was most unfair, because Jack was as helpless and frightened as I.

Then at last we came to the place I shall call The School. I do not know why Dr. Collins allowed us to flounder so long, but one day when I called him after weeks of dispiriting search, he asked if we had tried The School. "It's about the best there is," he said, and promised to write and send them a preliminary report so they would be prepared for our interview.

It was a welcoming place. Despite all our apprehensions and overwhelming sense of defeat as we sat in the waiting room, we felt that instantly.

Memory plays strange tricks. I don't know what made me think, while we waited there, of the day we had been married. How the world had glittered that day! If you loved each other and worked hard, if you were loyal and honest, life would reward you. It is just as well we could not have known the strange places to which life would bring us.

I looked secretly at the other faces in the waiting room. There was a handsome young couple with a look of security and position. Surely they never expected to be sitting here! Then an older couple, gray, shabby and genteel, she in a clean cotton dress and worn gloves; apparently life had not been easy for them, and you could tell they were bewildered, as if to ask why the extra burden had been put upon them.

Finally we were directed to a pleasant man, the psychiatric social worker who would listen to our story. He had already gone over the papers on his desk, the history of Tony sent by Dr. Collins.

We shook hands. "Our doctors have gone over all this," he told us, indicating the papers. "If you are still interested after we have answered all your questions, I believe we will accept Tony. He seems to be a child we might help."

And he explained, "We do not accept psychotic children here. Only the emotionally disturbed, those with behavior problems. We offer a tightly structured environment, with highly individual attention. The ratio of staff to students is three to one."

We sat there carefully listening and yet not really considering. We had already made up our minds. This was the place. There was an unmistakable warmth about the comfortable brick ivy-covered houses which lay scattered over the enormous meadows and sheltered behind old trees. At a bend in the driveway we had seen a pond where boys could swim in the summer and skate in the winter; from where we now sat we could hear cries from a ballfield across the lane. The slap of tennis balls came from the courts just below the windows.

". . . No one is ever left alone to sink into depression or get into trouble. Every minute is accounted for, between study and recreation. The staff people work in conjunction with whatever psychiatrist is attending any particular boy."

"What is the average length of stay?" Jack inquired.

"Anywhere from one to three years. It's hard to give an average. By the time we are through with them, which is by the time they have completed the high-school course, they are ready to go to college or to work or to whatever place in life the individual is fitted for."

Hope, irrepressible, began rising inside me again. "In other words, most of the boys really turn out well?"

"Yes, I would say so. You may wonder what it is we do. No magic, I assure you. But you see, by taking the boy out of the home where the whole family is so emotionally involved, and raising him in the care of impartial, trained people, we can inculcate a whole new set of living habits. It is a conditioning process which no parent, however skilled, devoted or intelligent could possibly effect."

That made sense.

"And so often at home these children resist psychotherapy. Here there is no choice about going. It is part of the weekly routine, like meals, basketball practice or math class. I note here that Tony has not seen his psychiatrist for the past few months."

"No, we have not been able to make him go. We're really in a pretty bad situation at home."

A sympathetic nod. "I can imagine. It can be rough on the family. What does Tony think about coming here? You've discussed it with him, of course?"

"Well, one doesn't *discuss* anything with Tony at this point. We told him, we informed him, that we were looking into this as a possibility. And he has flatly refused to have anything to do with it."

"He won't come?"

"No, I really don't know what we're going to do," Jack said, "if we can't persuade him."

"I suppose he will have to be brought forcibly."

"I suppose so. My brother, maybe," Jack said. There was a miserable silence, thinking about that, and then Jack asked, "May we discuss the fee?"

"Oh yes. It is high. It has to be, for what we give. The fee is six hundred dollars a month."

It did not mean a thing to me at that moment. If he had said six thousand dollars a month I think it would have made no more impression on me. All I knew was that we had found a place to take Tony, people to help him, and we would have rest.

They were to make room for Tony the following week. That was the longest week in my life. I literally counted the hours. The tension in our house built up so that it seemed surely something, someone, must burst open.

Yet the very night before we were to go, Jack would have changed his mind. Neither of us could sleep. We sat up late, whispering. Jack wanted reassurance, desperately. "Are we doing the right thing, Louise? Should we try longer?"

I threw up my hands. "How can we ask it of ourselves? Or the children?"

"I don't know. And yet—we have to give Tony every chance. We owe it to him."

"Jack, maybe they'll help him at The School. I feel so strongly that they will. We aren't doing a thing for him here."

"That's true."

We took Tony in the morning. Quietly, so that he would not hear and suspect, Russell and another man, the only other one who knew our story, parked their car down at the end of the driveway and entered by the back door, which had been left open for them.

Tony had to be taken bodily from his room, kicking, screaming, and most terrible of all cursing Jack and me for putting him out of his home. Jane and the twins had already left for school and mercifully were spared the scene. Hanna hid in the kitchen, wringing her hands. The two men got Tony into the back seat of the car between them; Jack drove. I drove the second car alone with all the luggage.

And so Tony left home.

I suppose we were all, in a sense, numb that

day. But The School held forth such hopes to us. Though I had not figured out just how, I truly believed that somehow they would know something no one else had known. I believed that in a year or two Tony would be straightened out; that he would come home and go to school and live with the family in peace. If I had known how it was to be I would surely not have been able to get through that day as steadily as I did.

I drove the car for two hundred miles, to The School. I met the staff and said the ordinary things. I knew what the right behavior must be. I knew I must manage for Jack's sake. Also, I must confess I had some feeling of relief, just the sheer physical relief of having a burden taken from me. That night I would go home and shut my door and be able to sleep all through one night.

We came home, exhausted and emptied. We sat down to dinner with our children. It was the first sane, quiet dinner hour in years.

The children talked of their own affairs; not a word about their brother was said. They were so young, and surely they could not understand the whole truth of what had happened. Yet I knew that they were aware that something deeply moving had taken place, and tactfully were trying to help their father and mother.

When we had almost finished the dessert, Jack spoke. "We are all thinking of Tony tonight. He's in a good place, a school where they will help him to get over his troubles. After a while," he said smiling at the three still faces, "he will be coming back to us."

There was no comment and presently they all

excused themselves to do their homework. Right afterward Jack and I went to our room and fell asleep.

It was at least a week later that I really understood what had happened. I was driving one forenoon toward the shopping center and there ahead of me on Maple Avenue I saw a boy. The shape and walk were so familiar that I thought absently: what is Tony doing out of school? Then I remembered; blind with tears, I had to stop the car. At last I knew my heart was broken.

Soon after, Tony wrote us a letter beseeching us to take him home. Jack answered it carefully. Very lovingly, he explained why it would be best for him to stay where he was for the time being. Tony's answering letter was a tirade of furious threats and hatred. Then no more letters came; there was silence.

Yet he came to feel comfortable at The School. Certainly he was more calm there. What we had been told was true. It was a happy place, as happy a place as could be built with boys like Tony. The boys were kept active every minute in mind and body, with no time to turn inward. If they did not improve, certainly they did not go downhill either.

The teaching and supervisory staffs were superb, from the house fathers and athletic coaches to the social workers, the psychologists, and all the various specialists in the education of disturbed children. A few of the best had received on-the-job training at The School. All of them had a marvelous natural endowment for their work. They had something more than sympathy, which any human heart should have, but which is never enough by itself. They had empathy, they almost knew what the boys were thinking and knew what to expect in any situation.

I think especially of one man, Tony's house father. Jim Walters was a calm young man from the Far West, with the laconic speech of his native region. His only training had been at a small normal school of no particular prestige, after which he had taken some courses in abnormal psychology. He had patience, humor and firmness. The boys knew they could trust him. Above all, he had unflagging energy.

Tony's insomnia plagued him at The School as it had all his life. Sometimes his tension was almost unbearable. Once, when Jim was on night duty, he found Tony pacing the upstairs corridor. It was almost two o'clock in the morning.

"How would you like to go outside and get rid of whatever's bothering you?" Jim asked.

Tony was astonished. Ordinarily it was forbidden to leave the building at such an hour.

"Yes, I'll stand and watch you, and you run up and down the lane until you've worked out all your trouble and will be able to sleep."

So in bitter, windy November Jim took a flashlight and waited in the cold while Tony raced down the lane again and again until his abnormal drive was sated. At last Jim brought him indoors, fixed a cup of cocoa and saw him into bed.

It was over a year before we were allowed to see Tony. Or rather, before he consented to see us. We were told that the separation trauma was especially severe in Tony's case because he had been so dependent upon his family, so utterly friendless in the outside world. He had made up his mind not to forgive us for having sent him away; he left our letters unopened on his shelf; boxes of cookies and baskets of fruit were allowed to rot. Finally we were told to make no further efforts until he indicated he was ready to accept them, and us.

However, we did make periodic trips to The School for conferences. We suffered, turning in at that gate and coming up the driveway, both hoping and fearing that we would see our son. But we never did. I am certain that the staff, with their usual efficiency, kept Tony occupied acres away when we made our visit.

The early reports during that first year were guardedly optimistic. The psychiatrist to whom Tony was assigned was an agreeable man with a vocabulary almost the replica of Dr. Collins'. I could have told him everything he was going to say before he said it.

Tony had "severe emotional problems." *A rose is a rose is a rose,* I thought wearily. I suppose I was very tired after the long trips and feeling the tension of being so near to our son and unable to see him. *A rose is a rose*—an emotional problem means that you cannot get along with the world, with other people or with yourself. And because you cannot "get along," and you behave badly, you are filled with guilt and are angry with yourself so you behave worse because you are so upset.

Then, of course, there are always your parents; and not because they were wicked but because they had problems of their own, in some way they failed to give you the love that a growing child requires. "The victim creates another victim," the doctor said, not accusingly but sympathetically. "It is all very complex, of course, living in a world in which old values are rapidly being lost, and no one is quite sure what will take their place. It is no wonder so many parents are confused . . ."

Indeed, we were confused.

A time came when we were told we could see Tony. We were to come for him at four o'clock, take him to dinner, ride around a bit if he wished and if things were going well, then bring him back to The School at eight o'clock.

We waited on the porch of his house. I could hear my heart thudding; my knees went weak and I sat down on the steps.

After twenty long minutes Jim came down. "Tony's fooling around up there with his shirt," he said, "but, of course, he's just nervous. I told him to take his time, that you'd wait."

Presently we heard hesitating footsteps on the stairs. A moment later Tony appeared in the doorway. Oh, he was older, not a child any more, but a young man, sixteen now, taller and so handsome, with a grace unusual for a boy his age. Not one of our children looked like him, nor was he exactly like either of us.

Jack put out his hand. "Tony," he said.

"Where's the car?" Tony asked, striding past us down the porch steps.

I looked questioningly at Jim but he only shook his head, forming with his lips the words. "Take it easy."

We got into the car, Tony on the front seat with his father, I in the back. He was well cared for, I could see, and that was good for my spirits. When he had been unkempt and dirty it had made him seem so sad, so beaten. Now, with a good haircut and a clean shirt he at least looked more hopeful, more in tune with the world.

We took him down the road to an attractive restaurant which we had earmarked on our several trips during the past year as the place where we would have our first dinner together.

"Hungry?" Jack asked casually.

"Yes."

We sat down at the window overlooking a flowered courtyard. I tried to feel like any ordinary mother out to dinner with her husband and son. I tried to feel that everything was normal and I was proud of my handsome boy. I was brought back harshly from my fantasy.

"I read a book the other day," Tony said. "It was in the drugstore. I stood there and read it all the way through."

We waited, alarmed by the severity of his expression.

"It told what good parents ought to be. It said that people get . . . the way I am . . . because their parents weren't qualified to be parents."

"Oh Tony," I began, but Jack's signal silenced me.

"I'm a miserable wreck, because both of you are, too. You're queers and you never should have had a child."

"In what way are we queer?" Jack asked quietly.

"You never played ball with me. All you ever wanted to do was tramp around looking at birds or read. Or work in the damned hospital."

"Well, maybe it would have been more fun for you if I'd been an athlete. I can see that. But I really don't see why that should make me such a terrible father."

"Read the book!" Tony exclaimed.

"Tony, there are a lot of things written in books, a lot of opinions that are inaccurate, distorted, or just plain wrong. Besides, I'm sure the book—"

"Listen, even the doctor that I've got here agrees! He says nobody's born with problems like mine! Afraid to talk to people, can't have friends! He says it's the way they're brought up!"

Jack swallowed. "I'm afraid I can't entirely agree," he said at last.

And if it is true, I thought—and maybe it is, maybe there is something defective in Jack and me, God knows I feel wrung out half the time— what good does it do to tell the child? He'll only hate us more and he'll never be able to breach the gap—it's cruel to talk to him like that. I felt so shabby, so inadequate, so wretched.

"You didn't really want me!" Tony cried. "That's why you rejected me!"

The waitress came for the order. Very calmly, Jack consulted with her. In a barely audible voice Tony gave his order for an enormous dinner and then I gave mine, although all appetite had fled.

When the waitress had left Tony resumed. "Don't think I'll ever forgive you. When I'm grown and out of this god-damned place I'll get even with you if it's the last thing I do!"

"Tony," Jack said, "You're a fair person. If there's one thing about you it's that you're fair and honest. Now, I want to ask you something. I want you to tell us what we have done wrong. Believe me, there is nothing in the world that your mother and I want more than to make you happy, to make you love us and get along together. The things you've mentioned just don't ring true. Tell us what we have really done wrong."

"You put me out of my house. You got rid of me."

"Tony, we didn't 'get rid' of you. It wasn't that way. We sent you here *after* we saw—surely you saw too—that nobody could go on living the way we were all living. It wouldn't have been good for you even if the others had been able to stand it, and we weren't able to stand it. Tony, you know that we've sent you here so that they can help you and then you will be able to come back home. We want you home."

"Oh, cut out the crap," Tony said; "let me eat my dinner. Shut up and take me back; I'm sick of looking at you."

Soup came, shrimp, roast beef, salad and dessert. Jack and I could barely touch them. Tony sat eating steadily and silently.

"My, it does your heart good to see a boy enjoy his food like that," the waitress said heartily.

We smiled wanly and finally stood up, paid the check and drove, still unspeaking, the shortest way back to The School.

Jim was waiting for us in the sitting room. "Well, Tony, how was it?"

"All right." Tony strode up the hall and out of sight, with no good-bye, without looking behind him.

We explained what had happened.

"Well, this is only a beginning," Jim said. "Don't forget, it's been a long time. Perhaps, though, you'd better wait a while before you come again. I think the doctor will want you to wait until Tony really asks for you. And he'll appreciate you and it will be more meaningful."

In all this time we had told no one what had happened to Tony. The public school knew only that he had been sent to a private school. Our friends and neighbors had been told the same thing. The only problem was he did not come home for Christmas vacation or in the summer. Certainly this must have appeared very odd.

For a long while I resisted facing up to the reason for our secrecy. My children, too, pleaded with us not to tell anyone about their brother.

Finally, one day after consulting Jack, I decided to bring the matter up. We were having lunch, and I quietly suggested maybe it was time to tell the truth about Tony. "It's becoming more and more complicated to live a lie, isn't it? People are surely wondering and guessing. Why not tell the truth and relieve ourselves of a heavy burden?"

With one voice the three protested. "Mother, please, for heaven's sake——"

"I couldn't face anybody in school," Jane cried. She looked almost terrified. "Have you any idea how the kids would talk? It's bad enough now;

they make cracks about 'the disappearance of Tony'; 'whatever happened to Tony?' "

"That's just it!" I said. "Let's end the mystery. After all, there's nothing to be ashamed of. Tony has problems, he's never done anything wrong——"

"Mom, you don't understand at all," Sarah admonished me. "Our friends would just make it a big thing to talk about in school!"

"Yeah," Freddy said. "Sick jokes. I could beat guys up when they made cracks about the nuthouse. Ma, let's leave things the way they are. Let people guess anything they want."

Sometimes I wish we had been completely truthful from the beginning. We are caught now in a tangle of lies, evasions which are painfully confusing to ourselves and which I am certain fool none of our friends. Yet at the start we had, I think, a valid enough reason for wanting to conceal Tony's troubles from the community. We really believed that in a few years he would be back in stride, perhaps at some Ivy League college. Nobody undeceived us; in fact, we were encouraged to believe this. Therefore we did not want to handicap a boy already shy and insecure by giving him a past to live down or by making him the subject of embarrassing speculation when he should return home. We lied to protect him, this I know. But like any lie, once told, it becomes almost impossible to untell even when you truly want to do so.

So Tony became a boy who had disappeared, a "lost" child whom no one talked about any longer.

Jack and I wondered often whether the other children thought about him very much. Strangely enough, Jane, who had suffered most from Tony, seemed to care the most. The first Christmas she came downstairs and offered me a package wrapped in tissue paper. She looked shy and self-conscious as though she did not want to talk, or could not.

"It's something I made for Tony. I thought if you were getting a package together you could put it in."

It was a muffler, her first finished product, just a simple stockinette stitch in bright red. Something about it, as it lay there inertly, seemed to speak so movingly that I was glad she had left the room so she would not see my tears.

Freddy seemed the least concerned, but then how can one really know? I remember the time he discovered the monthly bill from The School, which I had left on the desk beside my checkbook.

"All that! Six hundred dollars every month for him?" He was aghast.

"Yes, the kind of care they give is very expensive," I explained.

"You could send"—he figured rapidly—"you could almost send the rest of us to college for what he costs you."

"I know."

"You always say Dad's not a rich man. Just a workman earning his living with his hands. You always tell us that."

"And it's true. You father earns a fine living because he's highly skilled and terribly busy. We have nothing extra. If he should stop working we'd have very little. That's why I try to teach you not to waste."

"And you're wasting all this on him!"

"Freddy!" I cried. "He's your brother! We have to make him well. We have to take every penny we can and if we didn't have it we'd borrow it; we'd do anything to make him well."

There was a silence. Freddy swallowed hard. "Gee, Ma, I'm sorry. I guess I know what you mean. You know I hope Tony gets better. You know I do."

Yet there was truth here, too. Our expenses *were* shocking. I had not thought it possible that in this day and age so few ways could be found to ease our financial load. Since Jack was self-employed, we were not eligible for most group insurance plans. Shortly after the war, he had taken out a major medical policy, the very best policy available. When Tony's bills first came in, however, we found listed quite clearly under the heading of exclusions: "mental disorders." And even if we had been covered, Jack told me that the company probably would have canceled our policy at the next renewal period.

Because he belonged to a hospital staff, Jack was eligible for the hospital's group plan, but even that wasn't much help. The many and varied exclusions all seemed to work against Tony—short periods of confinements were covered but they were followed by long, nonreimbursed "waiting periods." Age limitations were lifted only if the insured was still in school. And all payments ceased if the head of the family was to die or reach age sixty-five.

I investigated one plan after another. I found that even under the most liberal arrangement possible—and even if we could have qualified—

Tony's expenses would have been paid only for one year and then to a maximum lifetime benefit of $10,000 for a single illness. Ten thousand dollars—a fortune to most people!—would have been no more than a drop in the bucket in our circumstances. And then, of course, these liberal benefits would be paid only if Tony were hospitalized. And thank heaven he was not sick enough for that!

I began to feel like an expert on the finances of mental illness, a very baffled expert. And I could not help thinking of all the parents, thousands of them with troubles like ours and no place to turn for help.

No place, I thought bleakly, except a state institution . . .

My head whirled with the enormity of it, the insolubility of it. I did not want to let myself feel so hopeless. Now of all times, Jack, I, the children, deserved some reaffirmation, something to prove to ourselves that life contains more than grief and perpetual worry. So, in the second summer after Tony's departure, the five of us in a rented station wagon, with all our camping gear, left home and traveled West for two whole wonderful months.

At first Jack resisted the idea. He said he couldn't afford to close the office, with expenses mounting; but I was firm—I said he couldn't afford not to go.

Truly, the family mended its wounds that summer. The foolish little squabbles that inevitably arise among three teenagers traveling thousands of miles were surprisingly few. More importantly, we did not mind them, because they seemed so normal.

We came to know each other. Camping on the north rim of the Grand Canyon we discovered Sarah missing from her sleeping bag. She had crept out to watch the dawn coming up over the rim, and there she sat, a dark outline against the rising splendor of pure rose and pearl.

There was the time we visited the Navajo villages, a world out of centuries gone, a clay village old in the time of Columbus. Jack had once made a hobby of Indian studies, to the twins' amazement.

"Gee, Dad, I didn't know you knew all that!"

"I didn't think you knew anything but medical stuff!"

It was the best time we had ever had together. All the tensions that poor Tony had caused were gone. I thought: Next time we'll come back and Tony will be with us.

8

TWO years slid past, slid quietly away before we knew it. Tony had one more year to go before graduation. Once again uneasiness began to stir in me. Where was the improvement we had been promised? He was still not able to come home for a visit. The doctors said he was still too hostile, that it would only destroy the progress he had made to allow him to have a brief taste of home and then be taken away again.

So we went to see him instead. The visits were no more satisfying than the first one had been. One day we were sitting in the car at The School when he suddenly demanded we take him home right then and there, that we just drive off.

"Tony," Jack said, "you know we can't do that."

"Why not? They don't own me. I'm not a prisoner here. I'm sick of the place."

"You will be coming home soon, I'm sure," Jack said very patiently. "But we have to do things right. We have to wait until they say it's best for you."

"The hell we do! You're trying to get rid of me. I'm going home now, do you hear me? Start that car or I'll—"

Tony was in the back seat; his father and I in the front. Suddenly his fists came down hard on Jack's shoulders. I cried out.

"Tony! You'll hurt your father!"

"You shut up and keep out of this!" He turned on me and, reaching for my face, streaked my cheek with his nails.

My eyes smarted with instant tears, more out of fright than pain. Then Tony's face crumpled; he began to cry. His fists pounded on his own knees.

"Will nobody help me? I can't control my temper and I'm afraid. Don't you see, I don't ever want to hurt anyone. Oh Ma, I wouldn't hurt you! I'm sorry, I'm sorry."

"Oh Tony, I know. Dad and I both know."

"Nobody does. Nobody understands!" he cried. "Nobody helps me. I can't control my temper and nobody helps me," he repeated. His head went down on his knees and Jack and I looked at that poor bent head. I remember everything with such clarity, the cold wind under the trees, the rushing sound of it there in that strange place where a father and mother sat with their son, who had been delivered over to strangers. I remember the stretching tendons of his thin young arms, the blond hairs on the arms of the boy almost a man, and so unready to be a man.

I remember wishing I might give both my own

arms, that I would do it willingly without a second's thought, to make Tony well.

On the long, desolate ride home we talked about something both of us had hidden from each other and even from ourselves. It was like removing a bandage from a wound, layer after painful layer.

"Jack," I said, "I know you don't want to talk about it, but maybe we ought to face it, maybe we'll have to—"

"Hospitalize him?"

"Yes. After what happened today I can't help thinking: he's not getting any better, is he?"

"Do you think he's worse? Do you notice anything new?"

"No. Not really. It's only that ... he's so sad. My God, so young and so sad." I had to stop. I did not want to cry. And I looked away, out at the speeding, sliding landscape as if there were an answer to be found out there.

"I know." Jack spoke very gently. "But at least, Louise, he hasn't got hallucinations; he isn't, as far as anyone can tell, a danger to himself or to anyone else. Yet. So far, thank God, there isn't any valid reason for locking him away."

"I meant for his health. I meant that maybe they could do something that The School can't do. After all, you put a person in a hospital to get well, don't you?"

"They can't do anything that The School can't do. It's psychotherapy wherever you go. And at The School at least he's free; he can walk to town for an ice cream cone. As long as he's able to do that I'm not going to put him away. Not until it's a last, absolutely final resort."

"Doctor Collins told me once that being put away in a hospital was one of Tony's secret fears."

"Why not? Dress it up however you want; all the gentle, understanding therapy can't hide the truth that you are shut away from the world of the really alive. Make no mistake about it. To many there's something frightening—almost medieval in its connotations—about the mere thought of institutionalization. Or so it would certainly seem to a boy like Tony, with his already unbearable frustrations and resentments. How fast do you think he would deteriorate?"

"But"—I persisted in spite of myself; I wanted to consider every possibility—"I've heard that with some it acts as a kind of shock treatment. They see these others—poor unfortunates who are *really* ill— and they are determined not to be like that."

Jack looked over at me. All he said was: "Tony?"

When you are in trouble like ours you turn to anything you think can help. You look for clues in popular articles or in scientific journals; you read everything in print. So it was that I began to notice with mounting frequency a number of articles in magazines and newspapers about the possibility of chemical causes of mental disturbance.

Tentatively, I brought the subject up with Tony's doctor at The School.

"Tranquilizing drugs?" he asked. "They don't work for everyone, you know. We have given them to Tony, also psychic energizers, when he was depressed. But in the case of tranquilizers, for instance, we had to give very large doses to produce any effect at all, and then the effect was only to make him lethargic. Now we have taken him off all medication."

That was not the type of chemotherapy I had meant. "I was thinking rather about some defect in the body's chemistry which makes people like Tony so disturbed in the first place."

"Oh. Well, I must tell you quite definitely that I don't accept that at all. Responsible psychiatry does not accept that. It's not chemistry, it's the environment acting on a defective personality that underlies these problems."

I had been reprimanded. Though I could sense that Jack, sitting at the other end of the table, did not approve, for once I was determined to be stubborn.

"I know that I'm not qualified to discuss scientific subjects," I persisted. "Still, I am Tony's mother, and I have read that in certain medical schools they have been doing some biochemical experimentation and that they have had some exciting results. Of course, it's all quite vague to me."

"Yes, and I'm afraid it's quite vague altogether. Results, like statistics, as we all know well, can be manipulated to prove almost anything you want to prove.

"Anyway," he continued, frowning slightly, "what do we mean by 'mentally ill'? I prefer to say that Tony is 'emotionally disturbed.' "

Jack cleared his throat. I knew that he was becoming impatient. If there was anything his

kind of mind disliked it was theory when specific
problems were waiting to be solved.

"Quite frankly," he said, "what has been worrying me is what we are going to do with our son
after graduation next June."

"Well, this is only September. Let's not worry
too soon."

"You don't offer anything after high school? No
possible arrangement?"

"No, we're simply not able to. But really I believe Tony will be ready for college by next summer."

Tony in college, a boy unable to make friends,
on the campus, in the dormitory, exposed to the
intense competition in which he could take no
part? It would be worse than the camp experience. I knew we were both remembering that.

"You hesitate. Why?"

"Because," Jack answered, "Tony hasn't really
changed since he came here. Oh, he has held his
own, he does his work, gets along under close supervision and care, and I certainly don't want you
to think we aren't glad of that. But you couldn't
really say he was any better, any more able to cope
with life. He can't even come home to his family."

"Well, I repeat, we have until next June; a lot
can happen by then. You'd be surprised, in therapy sometimes you go for months, even years, and
nothing seems to happen; then suddenly one day
it's like striking oil. Everything happens at once."

"And the patient is well?" I asked.

The doctor nodded. "You might call it that. I
would prefer to say, since it is always a moot
question as to what 'well' means, that the patient

sees. That he is able to accept himself. Once you have accepted yourself, everything else is that much easier. They're fantastic, the things that can happen in therapy."

"Well, of course we hope for that," Jack persisted. "But it is as well to be prepared for it not happening. I would like very much to have some other definite plan in reserve."

"Of course. We will have a meeting and look into possibilities. Then in a month or so, we will have a joint meeting of the psychiatric staff. You can be present and we will see what we can come up with for Tony."

We returned about six weeks later. Jim was coming down the driveway as we entered the parking lot. We stood and talked with him for a few minutes. He had a countryman's honesty; he concealed nothing.

"Tony's the same," he said, "the same as when he came. He doesn't talk much; he's tense and withdrawn. He does find relief in sports and there he really drives, pushes himself to get rid of his tensions."

"But he never makes any trouble?" Jack inquired.

"Oh no, not Tony. He's not like some. I've never had to call him down for a thing. He obeys all the rules. It would be a good thing if he would break out and do something mischievous for once."

"They used to tell me the same thing when he was in grade school, Jim."

"Yes, I know. I've seen the type many times, unfortunately."

"Then maybe you can tell us something. What becomes of them?" Jack asked quickly.

"Well, sir, it's not too hopeful. A lot of them get along here all right. It's sort of a cocoon here, you know, warm, protected. But they break down when they leave."

"Permanently?" I asked.

"Some. Of course, others go to a hospital for a while and then get out. Then sometimes those go back again, too. It's hard to say. Then," more cheerfully, "there are those who go to college. Some stick it out and learn to live with their problems, more or less. It all depends on what their trouble was."

"So you really can't predict very well."

"Not from what I've seen, no sir. It's easy to be fooled about who is going to make it and who is going to crash."

"And you've seen quite a few, I expect."

"Well, I've been here fifteen years. I've seen a few thousand come and go."

We shook hands. I had a feeling this was more objective truth than we had heard in a long time.

We had a considerable wait. The doctors had been delayed at a meeting. There was one other pair of parents in the tiny room. After a while we introduced ourselves.

They were middle-aged like us, probably younger than they looked. Her hands kept clasping and unclasping over a cheap, worn pocketbook. How can they afford this place? I wondered. Correctly, it turned out. "We have to take our boy out," the mother said worriedly. "That's what we're here to talk about."

And the father: "We've gone about as far as we can go. To tell you the truth, I'm strapped. I don't know what we're going to do."

"He can't live at home?" I asked.

The mother shook her head. "No, I suppose in my heart I know he never will. It would be unbearable, impossible for us and for him."

I could imagine. "We have the same trouble with our son."

"If we only knew what was really the matter with him!" the father burst out. "I get so confused! I've heard so much about what they can do in psychotherapy, and our boy's been having it since—when was it, Ada? Since he was in third grade! I've worked my hands to the bone to pay for it, I can tell you. I'm a boss plumber, I've got a little business and God knows I don't mind working. I'd spend every nickel and I darn near have. But it's been ten years and there isn't any change in him at all."

"If you ask me," the mother put in bitterly, "he's worse."

I nodded, seeing it all, exactly.

"And I feel so sorry for him, my own kid, not able to come home! We've got a house, his own room standing there empty. We brought him here last year; the doctors thought we had to because we couldn't stand him at home. We've got another boy and we had to think of him. But now I just can't afford this any more."

"So we're going to try the Y," the mother said.

"There's a Y in our city and they said we should get him a room there and try to find him a job. Maybe something in a gas station. Oh, I really don't know what. But what troubles me," she confided, "is that we have to do this when they've all been telling us that he needs what they call a 'structured environment.' You know, where they plan all the time, when to get up and when to go to bed? But when our boy is alone he turns night into day! He'll sit up all night doing nothing, just maybe looking at TV, or sometimes I've found him just staring at the wall. How long is he going to get along at the Y? A stranger with nobody to notice him, let alone get through the day? It won't work," she said, and her hands twisted on the purse; "nobody can tell me it will. Yet there isn't anything else we can do."

"It would be easier," the man said, "if he were in a hospital. But he isn't sick enough for that. You can't put him in one if he doesn't need it. And of course I thank God he doesn't. Yet."

There wasn't anything to say, except to murmur, "I know. Yes, I know."

When we were summoned into our conference they were sitting around a table: three psychiatrists and two social workers. So this was it. Here we were at a turning point again. My mind was back almost three years before to the time of our first visit when we thought we had found our answer. Now the three years had all but sped away and here we were again, where we had begun. Musical chairs.

"We are confronted here, quite frankly," the senior psychiatrist began, "with a certain difference of opinion. However," turning to Jack, "that won't astonish you, I'm sure. As a physician, you must see that happen fairly often in your field too."

Jack smiled politely.

"The question is what should be done with Tony. Doctor Lester does not share my more hopeful predictions for Tony. I am in favor of permitting him to try things out at home. He could go to college as a day student, since it is obvious he could not do well in a dormitory—"

My heart sank. Home again! What could the man be talking about? I wanted Tony home, but not like this, not this brooding pain, this bottled-up rage.

"—and Doctor Lester thinks—well, suppose you express your opinion, doctor."

We had never met Dr. Lester. He was a saturnine person with a very direct manner. "I've been seeing Tony for several weeks, very intensively. I have an entirely different feeling about him. I believe he is far more highly disturbed than would appear on the surface."

This man was more positive than anyone had been before. Surely no one would be so positive if he did not have facts upon which to base his opinion. Jack and I leaned forward intently.

"As a matter of fact, it is my belief that Tony could become violent at any time, his balance is that precarious."

"Violent, doctor?"

"Yes; when a boy makes the threats that he makes, I believe one has to take them seriously. I am not of the school that holds he may just be letting off steam."

"What sort of threats?" Jack asked quietly.

"Threats to hurt people. Me and other people here if we don't allow him to go home. You, if he does go home and you 'get in his way.' "

"Well, I'm now entirely in the dark," Jack said after a minute. "For years I've been hearing that my son was emotionally disturbed. Depressed. Passive-aggressive. A schizoid personality. But I have never been told that he was capable of violence. Has there been some change, has anything happened to bring you to this opinion?"

"You cannot pinpoint time or place in this field. The damaged psyche doesn't get that way overnight. I would have to do a great deal more work with Tony in deep analysis to ascertain that. I believe this is very deep-seated and has been with him a long time."

"I see. What shall we do with him, then?"

I marveled that my husband was able to speak, for I was stunned.

"Well, first of all, I suggest that you give up all thoughts of having the boy come home. Not even for an hour. And secondly, if he were my son, after he leaves here in June I would place him in one of the finest clinics in the country; I can recommend the one where I was fortunate enough to have my training. I believe they will help him there if anyone can."

"And you, doctor?" Jack turned to the senior psychiatrist.

"I disagree with my colleague. Tony is obsessive-compulsive, he is passive-aggressive. But once past adolescence and with continued therapy, of course, you ought to see marked improvement."

"But you have no other solution short of trying things out at home?"

The doctor shook his head. "There is no other place."

I spoke up. "Nobody has asked me, but since I am the one who will have to get along with Tony at home, I want to say that ... well, I'll need help. I'll need to be told how to do it. I can't even relate to him for an hour when we visit him here. How can I manage with him at home?"

"You will not manage at home as long as your pattern of rejection exists."

"My pattern of rejection?" My heart began to pound.

Dr. Lester opened his mouth to answer me, but he was interrupted gently and firmly by his senior.

"No useful purpose can be served by probing into areas that obviously cannot be changed. Our problem is of the moment."

There was a silence around the table. Then Jack addressed Dr. Lester. "This clinic that you speak of—you say there would be intensive psychoanalysis?"

"Yes. The very best."

"But Tony has already had so much."

"Yes, but not in the same way. He hasn't been ready enough for it, old enough. This would be much more intensive." There was a pause. "Unfortunately it is expensive. Twenty-five thousand dollars a year."

"Oh!" I cried.

The doctor turned to me. "You are surprised, I know. You would be surprised to learn that there is a waiting list."

"Then these people are a lot richer than I. I haven't got twenty-five thousand dollars a year, even for my son."

Silence fell again, part depression, part weariness and part embarrassment. Into it came the voice of a social worker, Mrs. Daniels, who had been, I recalled, most intelligent and most helpful when we first had come to The School.

"May I make a suggstion?" she asked. Everyone turned to her.

"Yes, please do."

"Well then, perhaps Tony's parents ought to seek some outside opinions about Tony's future. Suppose we were to supply you with the names of several of the best qualified men in the field of adolescent psychiatry; you could consult with them, perhaps you could find what places are available for short-term treatment in a sanitarium, if that should be necessary, or maybe something entirely different."

Well meant as it was, the suggestion was mere buck-passing. But it was still a good way to terminate the fruitless meeting. So it was decided that The School would compile Tony's records and send them to certain doctors whom we would then go to see.

During the next two months we saw five of them in a long pilgrimage by train, plane and car. Everyone was attached to some clinic or hospital and everyone of course suggested that we bring Tony there for an opinion. All of them, having studied the records, were in agreement that the boy had a personality disorder, but the degree of severity was the moot question. Opinions ranged from the possibility that Tony was indeed capable of violence to the mild view that he was merely going through an exaggeratedly difficult adolescence.

The last man we saw was the aged director of a well-known mental hospital. He was the most prestigious, yet he was the most forthright of them all, the easiest to understand, and the one who seemed to understand us best.

After we had gone through the familiar history, he said to us: "I know that the question which you want to have answered above all others is whether your boy can ever get well. And I have to answer you that I do not know. Exactly as we do not know exactly why he is the way he is, so we do not know whether he will always be the way he is."

Jack sighed. "What would you do if you were in our place?"

"First I would have him graduate from high school. At least he will have a high-school diploma. If there should be a recovery he would then have some tool with which to face the world. Then bring him here and I will work with him in therapy. Perhaps I shall be able to tell you more after that."

He was a gentle man with the tender qualities of the old and seasoned. But for all his gentleness and kind smile, there was no hope in this room either. What if we were to bring Tony here for psychotherapy? He had been having it for so long and we had got nowhere. Would this not be simply more of the same?

We thanked him and rose to go. But he was not

quite finished. "There is one more thing I want to say to you. I am sure you have a busy practice and I know you have spent a great deal on your son. But unless you are a very rich man"—he paused, feeling for the words—"well, you can impoverish yourself. I have seen it so often. I have seen parents deprive their other children and deprive themselves until it hurt. And in the end it made no difference anyway. Don't do it, doctor."

We walked down the long drive in the gray November.

"What was he telling us, Jack, about not spending too much? That finally and after all we may have to go to a state hospital?"

"What do you think?" Jack countered bitterly.

So we drove home through the lowering afternoon. Another day, another journey, another flare of hope come to nothing.

I must, I simply must, get over this persistent, naïve nourishing of hope, I lashed at myself silently. Here we had until recently been planning for graduation and college; nobody had given us any reason to think otherwise. On the contrary, we had been fed on hope. Now suddenly, matter of factly, almost casually, the word "hospital" was being bandied about. How had all this happened without our realizing it?

"Listen here," Jack spoke with sudden determination. "I'm going to take the bull by the horns. I'm going to make my own arrangements for an intensive study to be made in a hospital. I want a final opinion once and for all. I can't make sense out of anything I've been told because I get two different stories on the same day, and the same man has a different story to tell on different days. I want to know what is the matter with my son and what to do for him."

"How long would such a study take?"

"About a month or six weeks, I should think."

"I don't think Tony will go. I'm sure he won't."

"Then he'll have to be taken. We must know where we stand."

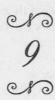

9

THE School was completely in agreement with Jack's proposal. I believe they welcomed it because they themselves had no idea what to do with Tony.

Tony's enormous dossier was forwarded again, this time to the hospital Jack had selected. Through the intervention of medical friends, Jack arranged to have Tony seen by Dr. Howard Brewster, whose name was known from coast to coast.

We ourselves did not speak to him on our first visit, since it took months to get to see him. One of his assistants heard our story, asked a very few questions and made no comment. Only when we were about to leave was he moved to speak and, while what he said was certainly discouraging, I had the feeling that he was being very honest.

"It sounds callous, but in many ways," he said, "the very poor are better off. They have no opportunity for choice so the decision makes itself. They keep the child at home and somehow live through it until they can stand no more or a crisis occurs. Then the public authorities step in and take the child to a hospital. But people like you spend years of their lives, their time, their money and above all their emotional investment going from place to place and in the hope of finding the answer that was not forthcoming at the last place. When the final crack-up comes the child goes to a hospital after all."

There was nothing to say. Everyone seemed to have decided that Tony would finish in a hospital.

Then Jack said quietly, "We have to try."

"Of course; you'll hear from us the minute Doctor Brewster has an opening for your son. It should be next month some time."

So once again Tony was taken against his will, this time by Jim. I must say The School did a fine job of calming Tony's fears and convincing him that this study was being undertaken for his own ultimate good. They told us afterward that, in spite of his fears, Tony responded with the dignity they expected of him. He walked into the hospital on the appointed day with his head up.

By the second week when we were allowed to visit him his head was no longer up. He had a private room in what is called a closed ward—a locked section of the building. All new patients under observation have to go there first. Later, when and if they are considered ready they are released into the "open section."

"Are you sure you can stand it?" Dr. Brewster asked us. I was puzzled, and he explained, "It is going to be difficult for you. He is going to beg you to take him home. And you are going to have to refuse him. Can you do it?"

"We have to," Jack answered.

We followed the doctor to the end of a long corridor. There, at a heavy steel double door, he withdrew a large key ring and fitted a key into a grim lock. No elegantly waxed mahogany, no sprays of gladioli in the downstairs lobby could soften the horror of this. And we were in one of the most "deluxe" mental hospitals in the entire world!

"Here are your parents, Tony, come to see you," Dr. Brewster said at the door of his room. "I've told them they may stay for twenty minutes."

Our son lay huddled on a bed in a small, bare room. Gone were the neat clothes he had worn at The School; he looked again as he had years ago at home when he wore the same shirt and slacks for ten days in a row. Only now he was a man except for the traces of adolescent acne on his face. He had salve but had apparently neglected to use it. His heavy beard had been growing for at least a week. His uncombed hair was greasy and his face twisted with hatred. I barely knew him.

"You god-damn bastard. Look what you've done to me! You think I'm crazy, putting me in here?"

"For study, Tony, you know that." Poor Jack, poor Jack, everyone leaning on him, depending on him for strength, blaming him, looking to him for the answers. "These are not crazy people. They are people with problems, Tony. Problems that can be helped."

"Yeah," Tony said. He swung up off the bed.

"You get me out of here. Understand? I want to get out of here today. Now."

"That's impossible, Tony," his father said gently. "You see, Doctor Brewster needs more time for the evaluation."

"To hell with him! I want to get out of here!"

"Tony, I want to get you out of here. But it's only for a couple of weeks. Tony, listen to me, you can understand; we've dawdled around long enough, we've got to set you on the right path and this is one of the best places in the country. I know they'll have the answers and—"

"Shut up, you son of a bitch! You put me in here, you signed me in, and now you god-damn well can go downstairs and sign me out!"

Tony's voice, never very low, had risen. The attendant came running in. He was a young man, beefy as a professional football player. "Come on, Tony," he said. "None of that. Your parents will have to leave if you're going to carry on."

Tony glared at him and subsided. He left and we stood there, not knowing what to say. Suddenly Tony fell back on the bed with the fight gone out of him. When he looked up his eyes were full of tears.

"Please take me home," he whispered. "Please. You say you love me; then take me home. I think of my home, it's so beautiful; maybe I've never told you how beautiful it is. I think of the view out over the garden in back, the birds coming to the feeder, and I keep seeing that print of the covered wagons over my desk."

This, this is more than any human being ought

to have to bear. Tear my heart out with bare hands and it will be no more than this.

"Tony, you will be home," I said. "That's what we want. Please help us; please help yourself! Try to do your best here for a couple of weeks; that's all it will be. And then we'll know what's wrong, how to—"

"How to get rid of my 'problems'?" He looked up mockingly through tears. "Oh, I can believe that!"

The attendant returned to the door. "The twenty minutes are up."

Jack put out his hand. "Anything you want, Tony, for the short time you'll be here? Books, anything special to eat?"

"Go to hell, you bastard!"

The attendant led us quietly from the room.

During the six-week period we made several trips for conferences with the doctor. We were not allowed to see Tony again. His words haunted me. Not the invective, but his eyes and his whispered voice when he had described his home.

"Maybe we ought to bring him home," I said to Jack.

He took my hand. "You know better."

I suppose I did. If even one of these doctors were right and he *did* become violent—even once. There were the other children to think of. Already they had had enough ugly memories, more than enough for a lifetime. No, it could not be done. I knew better, indeed.

Dr. Brewster had the whole sheaf of papers before him, that sheaf which had been traveling about the country, growing thicker as it went. He had read them all, for when we spoke to him he seemed to know every small incident in Tony's life, from his difficulties with sleep in infancy right up to the present.

He had many questions and he was patient with our questions. He told us that electroencephalograms had been made to ascertain whether there was brain damage; there was none. Batteries of tests had been made—I.Q., Rorschach, every sort there is.

"A child like Tony comes equipped, as we all do, with a certain kind of personality. Some are more able to withstand the shocks of life than others. That's self-evident. The environment acts, and in children environment means, of course, chiefly the parents. Sometimes the action just isn't good for that particular child."

"So then it *is* the parents' fault?" I asked for perhaps the thousandth time.

"Well, it is true in all these cases the parents are somewhat to blame. They are always somewhat at fault. But we must not oversimplify. Really it is the entire culture which acts upon the child. He meets others besides his parents, after all. Anyone the child may encounter at school or in the neighborhood may have a profound, sometimes devastating influence upon him."

Something had continued to plague me, and again I had to know.

"Doctor, you've read the history and you know that I used to work at painting when Tony was little. Do you think that had anything to do with—"

"Nonsense!" Jack interrupted.

"Not nonsense." Dr. Brewster was firm. "Certainly I don't think that was the core of the trouble, but there is a very complex interrelationship of all the factors in any situation of this kind. Without going into it far more deeply than I have had opportunity to do, it would be hard to say. Art might have been a form of rejection of and escape from a troublesome child. I do not say it was, but it might have been."

"Let's look at the present," Jack said almost peremptorily. "How sick is he? Will he be able to function, in your opinion?" he asked for perhaps the thousandth time, too.

"We'll know more when he has been here longer. Give me another three weeks. I'll keep in touch with you and by that time we shall have been able to complete our studies and have a better idea of the future."

So the six weeks came to an end. We returned on a magnificent summer day for a final summation and conclusion.

That's when we learned that Tony had paranoid schizophrenia.

10

IT seemed as though the world ought to have altered, as though this news should have made some visible change in things. But the day was still brilliant when we came out and walked down the driveway. The girl in the pink dress was still reading under the tree.

"At last and at least," Jack said, "we have a name for it. He's classified."

"Jack, don't be bitter."

"What should I be?"

"All these years," I reflected. "That's what you said so long ago on that day at camp, do you remember? And you were right."

"Pin a medal on me."

Schizophrenia. Tony was the same as he had been; the condition was the same, yet now that this name had been officially put upon it, I was sickened. It was one of the most sinister words in the language. Its connotations came with it: a soul continually at war with itself, without peace.

Well, now where? We had paid three thousand

dollars for this study and we had an answer, a final diagnosis. But still no one could tell us where Tony might live.

"I shall go back to Doctor Collins," I said. "Maybe he knows a place."

"You know what I think of him," Jack retorted.

I knew. *Tony isn't really as sick as your husband thinks he is. Go home and be firm with him.*

But he had been kind. He had erred, but at least he had erred on Tony's side. He had been optimistic, if foolishly so; he had wanted to give Tony every chance. I couldn't be angry at Dr. Collins; and maybe, just maybe, he might know something.

If he was surprised to hear the diagnosis he gave no indication of it. And he did not know of any facilities for schizophrenics who do not need hospitalization.

"Except one. Yes, there is one man down South whom I know of. It's a very unusual situation."

"What is it?" I asked eagerly.

"He's a psychiatrist who takes a few schizophrenic children into his home and works with them individually. He has been extremely successful with them."

"That sounds like what we're looking for!"

"Unfortunately, the fee is rather high. I don't know whether you— Well, it costs fifty thousand dollars a year."

"You can't possibly be serious!"

"Why? If you have the money I can't think of any better use to which you could put it than your child's health."

I was speechless. Your child's health, of course. But it shouldn't have to cost so much. It was so outrageously unfair.

"In any case," I said, "worth it or not, unlike some people we haven't got fifty thousand dollars a year."

But on the way home it occurred to me that fifty thousand dollars was no more unreal to me than the sums we were already spending are to the majority of people. It was all a question of degree.

Surely you will do anything for your child. But you have to live along the way. You have to take care of your other children who are not sick. They are entitled to their share, too. How much ought you to spend on the sick one? How ought you to apportion what you have? No one can answer that but the individual parent, alone with conscience. Some will say: "Everything for the sick one because the healthy can take care of themselves." Others will say: "The well have a future, therefore give to them; don't sacrifice them for the sake of the hopelessly ill."

It isn't fair to force people to make decisions like that. And how ironical to think that even if we had been covered by the most enlightened health insurance policies, we would have been *penalized* for not putting our child in a hospital—and then for a limited time only. As I knew only too well, for all practical purposes in a situation like Tony's there was no financial aid at all.

These psychiatric fees, these stunning, outrageous fees out of the Arabian Nights! Even for the rich there is no promise of definite results, no end in sight! I was shaking with anger by the time I got home. It was several days before I could even mention the fifty-thousand-dollar doctor to Jack.

And then we found the place. As I look back on that frantic search I realize that finding it was an utter fluke, a piece of what under happier circumstances you might call luck. No one in the psychiatric profession helped us or had even the remotest clue to any possible arrangement. It was Jack's brother Russell who stumbled across the lead, and we investigated it within the hour.

Russell had a friend, a schoolteacher, whose uncle was a psychiatrist. The latter was semiretired from office practice and with his wife, who was also a psychiatrist, had taken a group of young people, boys and girls, into their home as patients. The teacher thought they might have room for another boy.

These doctors, Robert and Millicent Johnson, lived about a day's drive from us in a pleasant seacoast town. On the telephone the husband told us he might be interested in Tony and that we could come to see him the next day.

At this desperate juncture what we wanted was kind, custodial care and nothing more. It had come to that. All I wanted was to see the house: Was it clean, cheerful and warm? Would Tony be well-fed? Were they good people, responsible and kind?

The answer to those questions was apparent almost at once. The house spoke welcome. The wife, as we came to know, was an amazing woman. She had never had children of her own, but she was keenly interested in problem girls and had written extensively about the subject. She was able to work with a maximum of six; her husband took an equal number of boys. They were a vigorous, athletic pair, looking much younger than their years.

The four of us sat on a stone veranda overlooking the water. The spreading sea-bleached wings of the modern house curved with the line of the low cliffs.

"I must confess," I said, "that ordinarily I don't feel comfortable in a modern house. But this seems to have grown out of the rocks."

Dr. Johnson smiled. "We love it, of course. My wife's family farmed here before the Civil War. We've sold off part and kept fifteen acres of waterfront. Perfect for our project."

Mrs. Johnson added: "The main thing is always to keep these young people busy. Here we can have boats and horses; adolescent girls especially adore horses, you know. Our boys and girls have to take care of everything themselves. They may keep dogs and cats, for instance, as long as they'll be responsible for them."

This is the place, I thought. I'm satisfied and Jack is too; I feel it. It was just as well; there was no alternative.

We had brought with us a sheaf of papers from the hospital giving the diagnosis and Dr. Brewster's comments. Dr. Brewster's name stirred great respect from Dr. Johnson.

"You won't have to see Tony?" Jack asked.

"No, whatever Doctor Brewster tells me will be sufficient. I shall telephone him for further details, but I am already satisfied from this report that Tony is a boy with whom I shall be able to work.

"I shall of course go into deep therapy. With all respect to The School, which naturally I know by reputation, you are aware that they do not have the time or facilities for the kind of work I shall do."

I listened with utmost attention and politeness. But inside I knew better. Deep analysis, "working through"—such hopes had finally gone. Kind custodial care would be enough. *Just be good to our son and keep him as happy as he is capable of being.*

Oh, by that time I could have reeled off the smooth sentences all by myself, exactly as Dr. Johnson was doing: "Too many therapists work only on the surface, trying to elicit a modicum of socially acceptable behavior. They never reach below to the underlying conflicts. Now, you have to do one or the other. You cannot attack both at the same time. There can, at least in my mind, be no question as to which of the two is more important."

"Certainly not," Jack agreed.

"We live in troubled times. I know, of course, that after all you have been through with Tony you do not expect miracles. You will not expect me to send him back cured next month."

We smiled weakly at the sad little joke.

"I wish it were possible. But these illnesses are a long time coming and they take a longer time to eradicate."

I sighed; I could not help myself.

"Yes," Dr. Johnson said, not without sympathy, "it has been a terrible burden for you both, I know. The world is a burden today if we allow it to be. You have to be strong to withstand the pressures of our society, the wars, the economic competition, the pace of change. It is the weak who succumb. We have to teach them to accept and live with it and with themselves. To live with their own disabilities, as it were."

"Well," Jack said, "there's no use hiding that Louise and I are infinitely relieved. You have come, both of you, like manna from Heaven. We have literally no place to go," he finished honestly.

"Yes, I know. My wife and I happen to find it a challenge to work with young people like these in close relationship such as you cannot have in office therapy. Living with them here, we see them exactly as they are. It isn't easy, but it is rewarding."

"We haven't discussed your fee," Jack said now.

"My fee. Oh yes, I shall have to ask you for a flat fee. Payable monthly. Ten thousand a year."

I tried to make a rapid mental calculation in terms of Jack's income. But at this particular moment in our lives money had almost lost its usual meaning.

"Should Tony be able to continue his education—and from what you tell me about him he ought to be kept mentally challenged—there is an excellent small college about an hour by bus. Tuition extra, naturally."

So we left, with warm handshakes and more cheer than we had felt in a long time. No matter what else, at least there was to be no hospital for Tony. No walls, no keys, no attendants. At least this was a home and he would have his room. He would come and go and walk down the street like a free human being. Driving homeward, Jack took his hand from the wheel and laid it over mine. There were no words.

11

YET, in the midst of the deepest human experiences of joy or grief, the practical always intervenes. The practical, naturally, is money. Without it this miraculous shelter with the Johnsons would have been impossible. We began now to add up what we owed.

Jack had a large surgical practice. He worked literally six and a half days a week, counting Sunday-morning rounds at the hospital until noon, not counting the nights, which were unpredictable. Out of his large income he paid large taxes. We had huge bills for insurance, larger now that Jack had bought a new policy to provide for Tony in the event of his death. We had three more children to educate. With this new expense there would be no savings at all; we would barely squeeze through.

We thought of possibilities. Jane was a good student; she would apply for a scholarship, if only a partial one. Of course all three would work during summer vacations. They were not capable of earning more than a couple of hundred dollars, but that would pay for their clothes and books.

Hanna—after twenty years I did not know how to say to her that the time had come. I could hardly get the words out, but I had to and I did.

She listened carefully, her gray head bent. For a minute she did not answer. Then she came over to where I stood beside the stove and took my hand between her two old hands.

"You couldn't get rid of me if you tried," she said, "you just couldn't. I've no place to go. I won't live with my two daughters-in-law and I'm not going to set myself up in a room alone. And I'm not going to work for anybody else."

"A lot of people would be glad to have you. They'd pay you well."

"No, I'm old now and I don't want to work so hard. I can't. I can't go the stairs and do things the way strangers expect. I'll just stay here and you and I will keep the house together and you'll give me a few dollars when you can. I don't want to live with anybody else. You're my family, after all these years."

And we *were* her family.

So we began, with our shoulders to the wheel. Jack dismissed his two office nurses. I practiced my typing, which had grown stale through disuse, and took over all the billing and records. We sold the second car. Our twenty-fifth anniversary came and went. For years we had planned to take a trip in celebration; I had never seen Europe and Jack had been there only during the war, but we knew without saying so that trips were not for us any more. Jack had belonged for years to a tennis club where he was often able to squeeze in a Sunday afternoon's exercise. Now he resigned, although the fee was low enough. "It's all the small things that add up, fifteen dollars here, twenty dollars there. We'll have to trim to the bone," he said.

And we did. Every month—and how fast the months rolled around—a substantial check went off to Dr. Johnson.

"For how long?" I asked once in desperation. It was evening and I was sitting at my desk going over the accounts. Now for the first time since we were very young, things were really pinching. Sarah's bill to the orthodontist was due. Freddy needed a winter overcoat and a good suit. Jane's tuition was owing. We had had to install new leaders and gutters, and that bill had just come in. Now Dr. Johnson had depleted the whole account again.

"How long can we go on doing this?" I asked Jack.

"Have you got any other solutions?"

"No, but . . . I keep thinking of that old doctor; do you remember the one who warned us against impoverishing ourselves?"

He put the newspaper down. "Louise, I don't want to hear any more about it. There is nothing else for us to do but to go on paying for as long as I am able. When I am no longer able, well, then we shall see what to do next."

I sighed and I wrote out the check. I thought angrily: For what? For a room, some food and a couple of hours of talk every week. It's not worth it. When I think of how Jack has to labor for his money, how he has to produce results in that operating room and not excuses! *But you need Dr. Johnson all the same,* the rational part of me argued. You know you need him. And he knows you know it, too.

Tony had finally settled down and adjusted to his life at the Johnsons'. He had of course gone there—under protest—only because he wanted to get out of the hospital and knew he could not come home. So he resigned himself, at least on the surface and in the beginning, to the arrangement. He enrolled at once in the nearby college and attended regularly.

"The tragedy of his illness is the waste," Dr. Johnson told us. "Do you know that his memory is fantastic? He can accomplish in half an hour what would take another student an hour and a half. But now that I live with and can see him in the daily situation, I realize how very ill he is. His thinking is delusional."

"For instance?" I asked.

"Well, as you know, I have to treat him like a small boy and insist he wash before he comes to the table. His clothes and hands are usually so filthy that he can really be offensive. The other night when I told him he would not be allowed to sit with us until he went upstairs to wash, he promptly left the table and refused his dinner."

"Went hungry rather than wash?"

"Well, you know he can't take orders, however politely given."

"Why is that, doctor. Can you explain?"

"It's because he doesn't want anyone to seem to have power over him. He has to feel all-powerful. So no one else can be permitted to have power over him, even in the most trivial matter. Senseless to you, of course, but *that's* paranoia."

"That is just what he used to do at home years ago. I never did know what to do about it and nobody ever told me."

"Yes, it is very difficult to handle. He is a very difficult boy. You know, I cannot go out of the house at night without finding another adult, some colleague, to take over for the evening. I simply cannot trust Tony here in the house."

"What are you afraid of, doctor?"

"You see, he is very unfriendly to the other boys and girls. There could easily be a fight. And I do not say that he or any of them would intentionally injure another one, but in these rages anything can happen. And of course I am responsible."

I wondered whether this meant that Dr. Johnson already wanted to be rid of Tony. "We are so grateful to you," I said quickly. "We are so grateful for your skill and kindness. I know it isn't easy for you."

One bitter winter afternoon when it was almost dark, as Hanna was in the kitchen and I was setting the table, the doorbell rang. It rang with a kind of loud anger through the house. I wondered who it could be at this time of day. And then I heard a little cry from Sarah, who had gone to answer the door.

There was Tony, framed against the outer dusk. I had not seen him in almost a year; he looked larger and lowering in the little entry. I don't know what I said; I must have spoken his name, but he did not greet me, just strode into the house, brushing Sarah aside without seeing her or anyone, and into the kitchen.

"Why Tony!" Hanna said with great aplomb. "What a surprise! How are you?"

"Don't bother me," he said. He went to the refrigerator, flung the door open and stood examining its contents. In the bright kitchen light I saw that he had come through mud and slush. His boots were sodden, the bottoms of his trousers stained. He wore no tie and his shirt was dirty.

"Would you like us to fix you something to eat?" I said, following Hanna's casual manner.

What had happened? Had he quarreled with Dr. Johnson? Was he in any trouble? But surely we would have heard of it from Dr. Johnson?

There was a plastic container of chicken salad in the refrigerator. Maybe it was slippery, or maybe the miss was deliberate: Who can tell? But it fell from his hand to the floor making a messy glob on the linoleum. It was followed by a dish of spinach and half a dozen apples, just tossed out onto the floor. Finally he found something that pleased him, some sliced roast beef on a plate. This he took and, sitting down at the kitchen table without removing his jacket, he began to wolf it down.

"Does Doctor Johnson know you are here?" I began mildly.

"You shut up about him! No, he doesn't know I'm here," he mimicked my voice. "And what's more he isn't going to know. You aren't going to let him know, do you hear?"

I felt my heart set up a very slow pounding in my chest. Hanna and Sarah stood transfixed.

Suddenly Tony stood up and came toward me. I

stepped back. "Do you hear me? You aren't going to tell him!"

"No, I'm not going to tell him," I repeated. "But won't he be worried about you?"

"He's got nothing to do with me. I'm not going to stay in his house any more when I've got a perfectly good house of my own. Now I'm hungry and I'm going to sit down here and eat and you stay away from the telephone, do you hear?"

"All right, Tony."

In the hallway, facing me but out of Tony's view stood Freddy, who had undoubtedly been brought from upstairs by the noise. He made the gesture of telephoning, raised his eyes in question and pointed upstairs to the extension phone. I nodded imperceptibly. To my vast relief I saw him move quietly away.

We stood there watching Tony eat. When he had finished the meat he went back to the refrigerator for some ice cream; then to the cakebox where he finished half a coffeecake; then back to the refrigerator to the cheese compartment. And all the time we stood there, Hanna, Sarah and I.

It is true I was frightened. But at the same time I was moved to pity such as I could feel for no one else in all the world. By his very anger it was as though Tony had thrown an unseen circle around himself over which no man could step. By the drawing it seemed to me that he had isolated himself from all human wants and love. I wanted so deeply to step across the circle; to sit down at the table with him; to pour a glass of milk for him and lay my hand on his shoulder; to talk gently to him. But this he would not allow. His anger would not allow it. And I was rooted, unable to cross the circle.

When he had finished eating he went into the living room leaving a trail of mud. Still in his outer clothes, he lay on the sofa, muddy feet placed squarely on the pillows.

"You stay here," he commanded. "Stay here with me."

Minutes passed. Tony closed his eyes. He must have been traveling hard all day, hitch-hiking, no doubt. Perhaps he would fall asleep. Sarah moved soundlessly over the carpet toward the hall. At once his eyes opened. "Where are you going?"

"Upstairs."

"Not to telephone?" he asked suspiciously.

"No, Tony. Just to do my homework."

He looked at her a moment. Something moved in his face. A memory perhaps, of a little sister with whom a lifetime ago he had played in the sand at Cape Cod. His eyes softened; they were so blue.

"All right, go on," he said.

I was still standing there when Jack came in. I saw instantly that he had been forewarned by Freddy.

"Hello, Tony," he said. He sat down on a chair beside the sofa. "I'm glad to see you."

Tony did not answer.

"But I am worried about Doctor Johnson. I don't suppose he knows you're here?"

"No, and it's none of his business."

"Well, Tony, it is. You know that."

"I don't know it."

"Come, Tony, you know that Doctor Johnson trusts you. It's a pity to break his trust by running away."

"Who cares about his trust?"

"I think you do," Jack said quietly; "I think you care very much."

Tony did not answer.

"Don't you think we ought to call and tell him you're here? It's not fair to frighten him when he's responsible for you."

"He's not responsible for me. I'm responsible for myself and I do what I want."

"Of course, you do a lot of things you want. You're entitled to at your age. But not everything you want. Nobody can do that. I know I certainly can't."

"Well, I can stay in my own home if I want to; that's one thing I can do. You have no right to keep me out."

"Tony, we don't want to keep you out. Someday you'll be back here. But right now you can't get along with the family."

"Then let them get out. You get out, we'd all be better off without you anyway. You get out and I'll run the house."

Jack sighed. It was hopeless to appeal to reason when Tony was like this. How many years had we tried and failed; would we never give up trying?

The long night passed. In the big leather chairs Jack and I dozed and woke. Neither of us wanted to go to bed and leave Tony lying there as he was.

The floor creaked. The furnace whirred on and

off; the clock bonged in the hall. Still in the jacket and boots, Tony slept on the sofa. There was an unreal quality about the night and this brief visit of the boy fleeing homeward; this one night in his parents' house after so many years, perhaps the last night.

In the half light I studied Tony's face. All tension was erased in sleep. He was at peace. If only that peace could carry over into waking! If only someone knew what burned behind the calm, high forehead: what twisting fire and corruption!

He was, fundamentally, so good. *A strong superego,* the psychiatrists said. "You could leave a fortune lying on a table and he would not touch a penny," Dr. Johnson had told us. "He's scrupulously honest, absolutely truthful." And he had said also, "You can tell how he has been brought up; underlying the hostility and the vulgarity which he so often expresses is a considerate, gentle young man who knows how to behave."

Here he was, on the honors' list at college: a reader, scholar, lover of music and art. What raged within him, what was the distortion, the fear that crippled him as surely as though he had lost a leg? In all the world, could no one tell us?

Morning came. I heard Hanna coming down the stairs into the kitchen. Then I smelled the coffee percolating. I was still sitting there when the doorbell rang. We all sprang up; Tony was startled out of sleep. Jack went to the door. It was Dr. Johnson. He must have been driving most of the night.

"Hello, Tony," he said calmly. At his signal, in grateful unutterable relief, we left the room.

For a long time we heard the murmur of voices in the living room. Tony's occasional protest rising, then subsiding. Jack had his coffee. The twins came down to breakfast and then went out by the back door to school.

I stood at the dining-room window looking at the bleak winter morning. Everything was varnished with cold. Birds clustered at the feeder, black flurrying spots against the whiteness; I wondered how they had passed the night.

Some time later Dr. Johnson came looking for Jack and me. "Tony and I are going to drive back," he said. "He agrees with me," he explained, raising his voice so that Tony could hear in the next room, "that it is best for him to stay with me for the present."

I took Dr. Johnson's hand in gratitude.

"Will you have something to eat before you leave?" Jack asked.

Hanna came in to us. "I've made corn muffins," she said. "Tony always liked them so much. Will you tell him we have corn muffins?"

Dr. Johnson went in to Tony and presently returned. "No, he wants to eat on the road. So we'll be going."

Now he would not eat in our house. Well, it was understandable. If we would not shelter him, why should he accept our hospitality? For that was what it must seem to him: hospitality, not his by right.

Tony was chastened, all anger spent. Quietly he followed Dr. Johnson to the front door. "Goodby, Hanna," he said, with his old courtesy. "Thank you for making the muffins. I'm sorry I don't feel like having any."

And he was gone down the walk to the car and out of our sight, this boy of many faces, this stranger, my son.

12

I COULD not sleep. Jack was exhausted and went to bed. I got up and walked through the quiet rooms which had been shaken with rage only hours before. I walked to the end of the hall, to Tony's room, and switched on the light against the gloomy day.

Everything remained as it had been when he was dragged away so long ago. I thought of a clock that stops at the moment of some natural catastrophe: there they lay, the artifacts of a twentieth-century American boy. Books: lives of the national heroes, John Paul Jones, Andrew Jackson. An Indian bark wigwam. A collection of stones from an expedition in fifth-grade science class.

What went wrong? After all the thousands of hours and millions of words, at what point did the road turn and could it have turned another way if we had done something different? Or if we had not done something that we did do?

The room is so clean and orderly. In the streaming sunlight or yellow lamplight, it is the best-kept room in the house.

We went through a bad few weeks. Dr. Johnson called to tell us that they had arrived home safely. But Tony had veered again to the extreme of despair. Understanding at last that he absolutely could not be allowed to come home, that the penalty for making another attempt like this would be severe and final, he was crushed.

"I sometimes think," he told Dr. Johnson, "that I would be better off dead."

I asked the doctor how seriously one ought to take the remark.

"You can never discount the possibility of suicide," he answered. "I don't believe that Tony has any present intention of doing any such thing, but patients of his sort, as you know, are very unpredictable. I would not want to tell you otherwise or be responsible for not having prepared you. Do you understand?"

I understood.

"In the meantime he is back at classes doing his work. I shall try to help him over this period with extra therapy as I see fit. So, incidentally, you will not be surprised at the extra charges on your bill. I shall watch him and do my best, you know that."

"I know that. Thank you, doctor," I said.

I began not to sleep well. A new kind of restlessness beset me. I lay awake thinking about Tony, remembering things that years before I had put away in the bottom of my mind and tried to forget.

*We had moved too often during his early years
... My tension during the prenatal period when
his father was overseas ... His father's preoccupa-
tion with his profession ... No strong companionship and father image ... A first child, and too
many other children coming along too rapidly ...
Our expectations were too high ... He had been
robbed of his rightful babyhood, had grown up too
fast ... Inconsistent handling ... Too permissive
... Too much discipline ... Oedipal fixation ...*

"Jack," I said one morning, "don't be annoyed
with me. I know I sound like a silly woman who
refuses to bow to the inevitable. Really I do know
better. But still I keep thinking that maybe
somewhere there is a man with a new idea."

"Dear Louise," Jack said, patiently, gently and
for the hundredth time, "there are no secrets in
medicine. No miracles. The world is small and if
there were any marvelous new knowledge it would
be all over the globe in a month."

And I would have gone anywhere on the globe
to find it.

"What does bother me, frankly," he continued,
"is not any wild ideas about cures, but a very
practical problem. What we should do if anything
were to happen to Doctor Johnson or if he should
suddenly just get tired of Tony. It's exhausting to
have him around, God knows. Maybe we should be
looking for an ace in the hole, while we still have
time."

And that was how we came to Dr. Davis. We
had no trouble finding him. His was a great name
in adolescent psychiatry, one of those we had
unaccountably missed in our long search.

His office was in a large eastern city. I went alone; Jack simply coud not spare the time. All we wanted to know anyway was whether there was a place for boys like Tony. And we really knew the answer to that already.

Once more I came into a book-lined room to confront a man behind a desk. As always he was armed with a pencil and notebook, and his manner was familiar to me, deliberate, listening and watchful.

Once more I went through the story from the very beginning: the psychiatrists, The School, the hospital and the evaluation, the life with Dr. Johnson.

"So now," Dr. Davis said when I had come to the end, "what you want to know is: 'What next?'"

"To tell you the truth, doctor, I really came because in spite of all I have been told, in spite of my husband's assurances to the contrary and my own common sense, I still have faint thoughts that maybe you know something no one else knows. But on the train this morning I told myself to get rid of these foolish hopes once and for all. I suppose then that I have really come just to ask you what other people do who have a boy like ours."

"They don't do anything. That is to say, there is no pattern. Most of them just keep the patient at home until something happens. Probably he falls apart, usually because the opposing pressures of the family and the patient set up an explosion. And then he goes to a hospital. That's about it."

"So that by keeping Tony where he is, in a controlled environment, we are really keeping him out of a hospital?"

"I would say that's probably true. Or saving him from drifting, at any rate. From the furnished rooms, the odd jobs and the eventual collapse."

The picture he drew was all too clear. Only the week before I had seen a boy on a bus, with frightened eyes, half pleading and half hostile; slovenly dressed, shoelaces dangling and tie askew. With my senses so sharpened, I watched him standing on the street corner as the bus drove away and recognized his hesitation, trying to make a great decision: whether to cross the street or not.

"My God," I said suddenly, "it's worse than cancer. At least, with cancer you can die."

Dr. Davis nodded.

I thought the interview was over. I reached for my bag and gloves. Why had I come all this way, taken another long tiring trip for nothing?

"Tell me," the doctor asked abruptly, "what do you know about schizophrenia?"

"Not very much. Nothing, really." Then the words burst out: "Except that it's the most baffling thing and it's—forgive me—nobody seems to know what to do about it except talk!"

"You're right. It is a *scourge*. One out of every hundred human beings in the world suffers from it at some time or other. More than a quarter of all the hospital beds in the world are filled with patients who have it. And you are right when you say that nobody knows very much what to do about it. Not yet."

"What about psychotherapy? What about it really?"

"It helps. It stabilizes a patient so that he can limp along with a crutch in a hospital or, if he's lucky and can find a place, outside of a hospital. And it may save him from suicide, although not always." He paused. "You probably know that schizophrenia is not always chronic. There are many cases in which people have an attack followed by a long or a short period of remission before the next attack. There are different types of schizophrenia and different degrees. It's interesting that a great many of these—in varying degrees —seem to get over their schizophrenic episodes without psychotherapy. About as many as do have psychotherapy, as a matter of fact."

"Then you don't believe in it?"

"I believe in it wholeheartedly! But only for neurotic patients and their so frequently neurotic families. For people who are 'maladjusted,' who need a new regimen of life and thought, who need to work through their problems. For them psychotherapy works. I myself make it work for people who have broken under pressure. They come out with greater understanding of themselves and greater strength than they ever had before. But we are talking now about schizophrenia, and that is something very different."

"How different, doctor?" I could hear my tense eagerness.

The doctor spoke emphatically. "Schizophrenia is a *physical* illness. Your son is as physically ill as he would be if he had diabetes. And his illness is no more your fault or anybody else's than it would be if he had diabetes. Schizophrenia," he said, "is a biochemical abnormality. Certain chemicals within these patients, very complex secretions of the adrenal gland, somehow or other fall out of balance. We don't yet know how or why. But we do know that there are marked changes in the behavior of certain people in which this imbalance exists. This 'changed behavior' is schizophrenia: a distortion of thought, of mood and perception. Of course, I am giving you the very simplest kind of summary."

I felt troubled, not wanting to accept anything so new and sudden too easily. "I have read reports in the newspapers from time to time. But they have been inconclusive. And besides, my husband always warned me against getting medical information out of the public press."

Dr. Davis smiled. "Of course. On both counts. News reports on medical subjects can be sensational and are often misleading. It is also true that there have been many false leads in this field. There always are, in any area of science. How long was it before the polio vaccines were perfected? But enough has been done on the subject of schizophrenia, enough clues uncovered by responsible investigators, to show that we are *on the right track*. In the best medical schools in this country, as well as in Europe, things have been uncovered that, taken together, form a discernible pattern. There are, for instance, some properties in the blood of schizophrenic patients which do not appear in the blood of healthy people. There are some different properties in their urine, also, all pointing to some chemical disturbances. These facts have been established, if not satisfactorily explained. Anyway, it's much too involved to go into here. . . . Did you know, by the way, that Freud himself once said that he and his disciples would have to work hard on their theories if they didn't want to be supplanted by the scientists with their syringes? So that even he, the father of psychoanalysis, wasn't entirely sure there might not be a physical basis for mental illness."

I was astounded. "This is very different from what I have been accustomed to hearing. We have always been led to believe that Tony's sickness is the result of a poor environment."

"I know. And I'm sorry. I have seen too many parents like you and I know how you suffer from guilt. There's always something wrong with the family, they tell you. It is too rich or it is too poor; too harsh or too lenient. Permissive, restrictive, overpossessive, rejecting, castrating. I know."

"Doctor Davis, I wonder if you can imagine what it is to live all these years remembering everything you ever said, every time you were angry or unsympathetic or impatient? Blaming yourself and wishing you could have a second chance. Wishing you could begin again in babyhood and do everything differently. 'Not enough love,' 'not the right kind of love.' But I know how I always loved Tony and how I love him now."

"If you could have the years back again, knowing what you know now, you would be more understanding, you would know that he was ill and could not help the things he did. Maybe you'd be more patient and less bewildered. But that wouldn't change him. He would still have schizophrenia. As for enough love—a schizophrenic child can never get enough love. You can tend him with every ounce of your strength for twenty-four hours a day and it will still not be enough. Children like these are a bottomless well of demands that no parent can hope to satisfy."

"That's true! One story, one game of checkers were never enough. Tony wanted hours, the whole day."

The doctor nodded.

"I could never reason with him. He made me do whatever he wanted. And I did it to keep peace in the house, a little peace for my husband's sake and for the other children. Sometimes I'd feel so ashamed to think how inadequate I was, to have had no authority at all—"

"Authority over a paranoid schizophrenic child! Of course not. Such patients cannot take direction; they must dominate because their fear will not allow them to let anyone gain even the slightest power over them. How can a mother handle that?"

"Is that why, even as a toddler, he always did the opposite of what he was asked to do?"

"Yes, he was sick even then. And as he grew older it got worse, didn't it?"

"Worse in degree, yet in kind the same. There has been no real change in Tony for better or for worse. Sometimes I wonder," I said, "whether he would have been different if we had not sent him to camp. He suffered so that summer. Maybe he would not have fallen entirely apart."

Dr. Davis shook his head. "No, if it had not

been that it would have been something else. Life itself, just living with people, is too much pressure for him to cope with."

"Why is he able to function to a fair extent where he is, but not at home?"

"It's understandable to turn against the ones you love best. Think about it a little. Love and hate are very close. The family is the repository of all this boy's memories of inadequacy and failure, of his first awareness of feeling that the world is a hard place to live in. He knows perfectly well that he is 'different.' If, as you say, he is exceptionally intelligent he is able to understand that he is very ill. Whom is he going to blame when frustration gets the better of him? Who else but the parents who brought him into the world? Particularly since —and this is the gravest injustice—so much of psychotherapy is taken up with showing how a poor parent-child relationship is at the root of all the trouble."

"Doctor," I wondered aloud, "why have we never been told all this before?"

"I suppose because the psychiatrists with whom you happened to come into contact hold the still prevailing view: that schizophrenia is caused by faulty childhood environment. Old ideas die hard, you know."

"But what about the experiments you just mentioned?"

"I'll tell you. At a certain great center recently where some very thought-provoking and obviously significant results were obtained, the Old Guard rejected them as products of 'wish fulfillment' on the part of the biochemists who made the experiments." He shook his head. "There have been errors; there will be more. It's true that the chemical experiments have not always produced uniform results and the dissenters have seized on that. But nothing in science ever comes prepackaged and flawless. Not the satellites or the moon shots or the polio vaccines I mentioned before. But we are on the right track and more and more psychiatrists are beginning to change their thinking."

I asked whether there would be more schizophrenia as life became more complicated.

"No," Dr. Davis answered. "Here's the striking truth. The percentage of schizophrenics in all society is the same. In the most primitive communities and in the most competitive, sophisticated, cosmopolitan cities. The stress theory that we've all read so much about, twentieth-century tension, cultural exclusion of the underprivileged, the shock of sudden emergence into a mechanized world—it all sounds very persuasive. But the facts are that schizophrenia occurs in the same proportion, about one in every hundred, as I said, among the rich and the poor and the ignorant and uneducated, in the jungle and on the streets of London and New York. That rather upsets the stress theory, I would say."

"One more question, please, if I may. It it hereditary?"

"If you mean: Does the child of a schizophrenic parent always have the disease? The answer is definitely no. But there certainly is a tendency for it to strike again and again in any one family; statistically there is evidence of that. And that again points to a genetic factor."

Dr. Davis rose and I knew the time was up. "If you want to know more I can give you the titles of a few books that may cast some light on the subject for you."

"Thank you," I said. "Thank you for everything."

"I wish you had something to thank me for. It is a scandal that there is nothing I can tell you to do now for your boy. It is shocking that there is no provision for patients like him, no living arrangements at all. You are fortunate that you were able to find a place and that you can manage to pay for it, even at great sacrifice."

We shook hands. "Go home and do the best you can, as you have been doing. And let's hope that people will pour funds into research so that we can make up for all the years when we did nothing but talk about it."

Once outside I wanted to put my head down and cry. This man who had after all been able to offer no solution had done me the greatest kindness. He had relieved me of the burden which had lain so heavily upon me through all the days and nights of these long years: the burden of worrying whether somehow, deep down, Tony's sickness was my fault. Now suddenly, I had met a man who believed in me. He believed that I loved my son, that I was not a defective monster who had brought a child into the world and ruined him.

I knew this was the kindest thing anyone had done for me in all my life.

13

THAT was three years ago. Since then the ideas I had first heard from Dr. Davis have become much more widely talked about.

In research centers all over the country, at Tulane, at Yale, at Harvard, to name only a few, doctors, psychologists and biochemists have been picking away at the wall of mystery which encloses schizophrenia. Certain chemicals compounded of body hormones have produced the symptoms of schizophrenia in well subjects. The natural response is the question: Can the process be reversed? As yet it has not been. But there is so much research going on throughout the world—in Saskatchewan, in Sweden, in Germany, in South Africa—that even a totally ignorant layman like me cannot help but foresee the inevitability of a breakthrough.

Rarely a month passes without the appearance of some item in the news, some clue, whether here or in Europe, any place where people are trying to solve the puzzle. Most rewarding to me is to see the scientific community admitting, indeed proclaiming, that schizophrenia has a physical cause. I began to clip these items. I read the books that Dr. Davis had recommended and, to my frequent pain, my son Tony came alive on the pages.

I began to note a pattern in the disease, common to all sufferers whether in greater or lesser degree.

For example: Schizophrenics, I read, very often have abnormal hearing ability. That had been our experience with Tony. I remember once being scolded by Jack because of it. I had been talking to him in very low tones about Tony; we were in the den and Tony was on the porch two rooms away. Suddenly Tony flung his books on the floor and, plunging across the hall, began to berate us for talking about him. I thought it had been a wild guess on his part, so I said soothingly we had been discussing something entirely different.

"You were not. I heard everything you said!" And he told us exactly what I had just said. I would not have believed it possible.

"I've warned you that his hearing was abnormally keen," Jack said afterward.

Imperviousness to pain. Yes, that was Tony. The time he had broken his arm and seemed not to feel it. We had been astounded and puzzled.

Imperviousness to cold. All the agonizing winter mornings when he had gone out into the New England snow dressed in shirt and slacks.

A conviction that other people were watching him. Tony had resented people's gaze. Many a crisis at the dinner table occurred because he accused somebody of staring at him. "Where am I supposed to look?" Sarah used to demand. "You sit across from me and when I raise my eyes from the plate they see you. What am I supposed to do?" Tony used to think that people on the street were staring at him too. He said he dreaded the walk to school because people turned to see how his hair was combed or whether his shoelaces were tied.

Overeating or loss of appetite. Tony's stupendous, constant desire for enormous quantities of food had amazed us. He could eat a large pie with a quart of milk right after a huge dinner.

I learned from my reading that we are apt to confuse the true withdrawal of the schizophrenic child with the shyness of the immature child who would rather stay home than go to a party. They are not the same at all. The schizophrenic is often withdrawn because he has aberrant thoughts which frighten him. He can hear voices in his head or see distorted faces and people who look much larger or smaller than they are supposed to be. Yet at the same time he often knows that these things are not true, that he is imagining them. But he cannot control his imaginings. He is filled with vague fears that people are against him, that they are perhaps trying to poison him. Again, he knows that there is no sense in his fears. Then he becomes afraid of himself.

Yes, during the last year at home Tony had prepared his own food or bought sandwiches at the delicatessen. He had been afraid to stay downstairs alone, afraid to stay in his room with the door closed.

I read about baseless inferiority and similarly

unfounded wild ideas of personal grandeur. Yes, there had been times when Tony had made the most embarrassing, absurd claim: "Anybody can be a concert pianist if he makes the effort; I know I could. I know I could be a championship tennis player if I practiced enough. You can do anything as long as you have the will. Nothing can stop you." Then there had been the times when he had wrung his pitiful hands, cursing himself for being worthless, no good for anything at all, better off dead.

Of course he had long known he was sick. Now I could understand the uselessness of offering euphemisms to patients like him, the foolishness of telling them that they "have problems." I could understand how this sort of remark could bewilder the patient who knows only too well that he has "problems." And I thought of how when he was only twelve years old and a patient of Dr. Collins, Tony had complained: "I like Doctor Collins, he's nice, but he doesn't help me at all. He really doesn't know what's the matter with me." Indeed, he had not known.

Inevitably, living at a university medical center, we had a good deal of social contact with doctors, psychiatrists among them. Whenever they were gathered at parties or meetings, Jack and I had avoided their discussions of mental illness; the subject was too painful. Now, however, I began to listen. Something that astonished me, in spite of Dr. Davis' statistics, was the number of people who either had had personal experience with schizophrenia or who knew someone with the problem. Several times I found myself asking about progress in chemical research. Again and again I was met with disagreement, sometimes condescending, sometimes arrogant.

"When I see them, then I'll believe them," one psychiatrist answered shortly, "all these laboratory miracle cures."

A pediatrician was not so easily put off: "What about the work with nicotinamide? I understand that the men who discovered it have had some remarkable results with schizophrenic patients—"

"The men who discovered it! Then how come it didn't work when other people tried it! Even the discoverers themselves have admitted it may not be the final answer—"

"But still, it may be a valuable breakthrough. And there are others. Taraxein and—"

"Breakthroughs! Rainbow-chasing!" This from a well-known analyst. "You cannot get away from the fact that it all starts with the family. Not only that, but I'll tell you something interesting." He turned to a rapt circle of listeners. "Some families actually do not *want* the sick member to get well. They need his sickness as a scapegoat for their own ills. I can recall one mother who had a heart attack as soon as her child showed signs of real improvement."

"I'd like to ask him why it doesn't make more sense to assume that the mother had the heart attack because of all the worry she'd been through," I whispered indignantly to Jack.

He pulled me away. "Don't upset yourself. You won't change his mind."

But I just couldn't understand such an attitude, and I told Jack so later! "Most doctors want to see new ideas. But these Freudians—they seem to want to hear their old ideas reaffirmed. It is almost as though they fear any change. Oh, I know there have been modifications, differences of opinion, but the basic thesis—certainly with regard to schizophrenia—has remained unchanged."

"Medicine is no different from any other field," Jack said. "The conservative establishment is strong. Too many advances have been hard-fought over bitter opposition. Take Semmelweiss. A century ago in Vienna he was laughed out of his hospital because he said that child-bed fever—and remember that more than ten percent of all mothers died of it in those days—was spread by the doctors themselves who didn't wash their hands between patients. And they laughed at him, broke him! After he died came Lister with his antisepsis and it was clear that poor Semmelweiss had known what he was doing. No, people do not accept new ideas easily, especially people who have spent a lifetime with one conviction."

"But we read so much about chemotherapy! Why, except for Doctor Davis, have we never run across any psychiatrists who believe in it? Even at the hospital!"

"Because," Jack said, "the chemotherapists are usually in research centers and not found seeing patients in practice. The men you meet are in practice and have their vested interests."

Time passed quietly enough at Dr. Johnson's. We heard no more from Tony. It was as though we had gone out of each other's lives. Two or three times a month we had a telephone conference with the doctor.

"Tony is entering very well into therapy," he reported. "We have established a working relationship. He is beginning to see himself more realistically."

Some of the comments were heartbreaking. "Tony said today that he is so worried you will die before he has learned to get along normally with you." Or this: "Tony has been reading about the work being done on schizophrenia in chemotherapy. He feels that what I am doing with him cannot really help much."

"And how did you answer that, Doctor Johnson?"

"I told him we are making very fine progress in our psychotherapy."

Perhaps they were. Tony was continuing to function at college He had always had a marked talent for languages and was now embarking on Russian, his fourth language. That was fine because it occupied his active mind and kept him in touch with the world.

But the answers to some of our other questions were less satisfying.

"Does he keep himself clean?"

"Unfortunately, no. He has to be shamed into taking a bath only when he smells so unpleasant that no one will sit next to him."

"Has he made any friends?"

"No, he is still all alone. He comes back from classes, goes to his room and studies."

"Does he eat at the table with the household?"

"Sometimes. But mostly he likes to prepare his

own food in the kitchen. He still is suspicious of others preparing his food. He fears being poisoned."

Exactly as he had at home, five, six, seven years ago. So I had no illusions. Year after year of psychotherapy, and in the most important areas, no change.

Still one had to look at it positively. Without psychotherapy, that is, without the crutch, the kind friend, the listening ear, the safety valve, whatever else you want to call it, Tony would surely have been far worse. Very likely he *would* have disintegrated. What Dr. Johnson was doing was to hold the line, a lifeline for a drowning man and something to grasp when the panic sets in. That is all it was. Not enough, but the best there is in the world today and much to be grateful for.

Toward the end of the second year at Dr. Johnson's, Tony started showing signs of discontent. He began to talk of going away.

"This may have started because I have had to reprimand him lately on account of his temper. He and one of the boys here have been fighting over the television set. Tony's rages become too violent and one day he threw the other boy on the floor and frightened him out of his wits. I had to be rather severe with him and he has been sulky toward me ever since. It may be that, or it may just be he is restless. He sees other boys growing into independence and self-sufficiency."

"What does he want to do?"

"He wants to leave college and get a job. He says he can take care of himself and he wants to see what life is all about. Ordinarily I would say that's a pretty healthy desire. But in Tony—"

We were having a three-way telephone conversation, I on the extension. I heard Jack say, "You haven't asked me, but in Tony I would think it was another indication of his paranoia, his unwillingness to accept authority. Of course, I am not a psychiatrist—"

"You may be perfectly right, all the same. The thing is, what to do about it?"

"Well, I would say"—and I thought I detected astonishment in Jack's tone—"I would say he had to be told he may not go. He obviously isn't fit to go."

"Well, that's easier said than done. You see, if I oppose him too strongly he will turn from me and I will lose the relationship we have built up during the last few years."

"Then you are really thinking of allowing him to leave?"

"Naturally I am trying to dissuade him. At least I want him to finish the semester so as not to lose his credits. Then, after that . . ."

"We'll cross that bridge when we come to it. Perhaps he'll have changed his mind by then."

When we hung up Jack said: "The plain fact is that this man has lost control of Tony. If Tony wants to go now nothing and no one will stop him."

14

ABOUT three weeks later at six-forty-five in the morning our telephone rang. Jack answered. I heard a sudden tightening in his voice, an impatient haste.

"Yes? When was that?"

I knew he was not talking about a patient. Something had happened to Tony.

"I'll be in my office all day. You can reach me there. And Louise will stay home and keep the telephone open. All right, yes, I know. God knows we ought to expect anything. All right, thanks; call us the minute——"

He hung up and turned to me. "Tony didn't come home last night. He left the house right after supper and Doctor Johnson thought perhaps he had come here."

"Maybe he's on his way."

"I know. Don't leave the house. I wish I could stay home. I wish I could cancel my office hours."

"Don't worry about us. Freddy and Sarah won't

be home all day and you don't have to worry
about me."

"I do worry about you. I don't want you to get
into an argument with Tony, do you hear? Don't
answer him back, no matter what he says. Don't
contradict him."

He moved from the shirt drawer to the tie rack
in an agitated pacing. As for me, my heart was
pounding. What if Tony had finally broken down?
What if he had decided to come home and, this
time, not allow himself to be led away again? I
could imagine him coming in as he had so often
done before: bursting like a bullet through the
door; the heavy, enraged tread that set the very
crystals on the chandelier trembling; doors slam-
ming.

Then something else came to mind that was far
worse, and then I hoped he really might be on the
way home. "Jack, could he . . . could he have done
something?"

"Killed himself?" Jack said roughly. "I don't
know. Don't you see that I don't know anything?" He swung around. "Louise, we'll get
through it. Please, you'll be all right, won't you?"

"Don't worry."

Freddy and Sarah left for school without being
told anything. It was Hanna's day off. In one way I
was sorry to be alone but in another way I was
glad to be free of her fearful, morbid predictions.

That was the longest day. Jack telephoned almost every hour. The doorbell rang, but it was
only a young man selling magazines. I was short
with the three or four friends who called; in order
to keep the telephone open I pleaded late for an

appointment with the dentist. One of my friends, a woman of whom I am ordinarily very fond, was much distressed because her new carpeting had just been delivered and the green was much brighter than she had ordered. Although on most days I could have sympathized with her, on this day I put the receiver back with a certain grim contempt.

By late afternoon it was obvious that Tony was not headed toward home. Where, then, had he gone?

Jack arrived earlier than usual, having canceled as many of his appointments as he could. The twins came home from school and had to be told. Nobody was hungry. I made an omelette hastily and set it on the kitchen table. The telephone rang, that crouching black instrument like a living voice of Fate.

It was Dr. Johnson. "There's a suitcase missing," he said, "a small tan overnight bag that belonged to Tony's roommate. And his electric razor is gone. But he didn't take much clothing."

"What about money?"

"You know, I've been adding things up. I had been wondering about the money you sent Tony for a new overcoat. I've been asking him about it and he has been promising to go downtown to buy it along with a few other things he needs. He must have been saving that money up. He might have a hundred and fifty dollars by now."

"Enough to go to California."

"Not to last very long."

But if he had taken the suitcase and money then he wasn't planning to ... do anything to himself. He wouldn't have brought money and an electric razor, would he?

Jack now took the telephone from me. I could hear Dr. Johnson repeating what he had already told me. Sarah and Freddy sat very still.

"What do you think we ought to do?" Jack asked Dr. Johnson. "Should we send out an alarm or should we wait another day or so?"

"Not the police," I whispered suddenly. "Oh, not the police!"

Strange how one's mind functions even in grief. I was still able to think: if the police are called it will be in the newspapers and then all the girls in Jane's dormitory at college will read it. And here in town everything will be out in the open, all the protective covering torn rudely away from the family; we can't do that.

And then I thought: Tony was wandering somewhere; maybe he didn't know who he was; maybe he really had lost his mind; maybe he was cold and frightened. He was no match for the world; he could be robbed, mugged . . .

"Get the police!" I cried out. "Find him—Jack, find him!"

He motioned me to silence. Sarah stood up and put her arm around me. Never before had I felt the need of my own child's security. But Sarah was a young woman now.

"Thank you, Doctor Johnson, thank you," Jack said, "we know you'll do everything. We'll leave it to your judgment." He hung up.

"Doctor Johnson doesn't think we ought to notify the police. He thinks that Tony may simply have gone off to get a job after all. Anyway, he thinks it would be a terrible experience for him to be picked up by the police and brought into the station house. It might do such harm as couldn't be undone. He would surely hate Doctor Johnson for it and there would be no trust between them after that." Jack sat down heavily. "Well, from what little I know, that makes sense, although who in God's name ever knows what does really make sense? Everything we've ever done seems to have been wrong."

"Oh, I wouldn't say that—"

"No matter. Let's wait a few more days. I wish you had something to do," he said suddenly. "Something to take you out of the house. Thank Heaven I won't have time to think tomorrow, I've got such a big day. It's a lifesaver, being overworked."

On the fourth day, just about when we were not sure how much longer we could hold on, the telephone brought news. It was Dr. Johnson.

"The mail's just come and there's a postcard from Tony in San Diego! It says 'I have a job and will write to you again. I don't need anything. Tony.'"

"Is it possible? Do you believe it?"

"Anything's possible. As I suspected, he wants to prove his own strength. If he can manage this it may be a breakthrough. If he can do this on his own it may be the start of a long upward trend."

"I'm afraid I don't think this proves anything except what we already know, that Tony's awfully sick," I said slowly. "What's rational about running off like this, worrying everyone to death, going away without plans, without knowing a soul? Without clothes? It's just not the way peo-ple do things."

"Not the way you do them. Or most of us. But you must remember that for Tony those things don't matter. He doesn't think in our terms at all. If he can get up enough courage to survive among strangers and make his way somehow, any-how, I for one will be vastly encouraged."

"I won't."

I did not mean to be rude or contradictory but I was terrified. And impatient with theories. "I want to get him back. I can't rest thinking of him alone in a strange city with nobody to turn to."

"Here's something that may be of help," Dr. Johnson said. "There's a young man I knew a few years ago, a psychiatric social worker at one of the hospitals. The last I'd heard he'd gone to San Diego. I think maybe I could trace him and ask him to stand by in case there should be any trou-ble."

"I wish you would. I'd feel a great deal better."

"All right. I'll try to get hold of him. But in the meantime, you must try to take a hopeful view. This may turn out to be a valuable experi-ence."

But there was only fear, no hope in us. Neither Jack nor I had much confidence any more in the power of experience to change our son.

So we waited. A week went by, probably the longest week we had ever known. Still, in a way, as one day was added to another without news of disaster, it seemed a good sign. Tony had been out in the world among strangers and nothing bad had happened yet.

Dr. Johnson called to say he had traced his friend through a social agency. He had spoken to him about Tony and the man had promised to help if he should be needed. In the meantime Dr. Johnson recommended that we do nothing.

Doing nothing is the hardest of all tasks. Through our minds, unspoken, went all the predictions and warnings we had heard through the years of travail. Thoughts of suicide, brought about by despair and loneliness. Fears that Tony might fall into bad company. That in his naïveté he might unwittingly be drawn into trouble of some kind. Fears for his physical well being. Of getting into a fight somewhere, touched off by a real or fancied insult.

The annual hospital banquet for the staff came along about midway during Tony's second week away. Certainly we were in no mood to go.

"But we have to go," Jack said. "We still have a family to support, and it would look very strange if we did not go."

All I remember about that dinner was being seated across from a woman who kept insisting that we ought to persuade our eldest son to study medicine. She was the wife of a busy doctor; they had only daughters, which seemed to disappoint her sorely, and she assured me that in our place she would bring influence to bear upon Tony to be a doctor, that he would never regret it.

Yet one manages to get through even such evenings. After endless hours we got home, to find a note on the hall table from Sarah: "Call Doctor Johnson no matter what time you get in."

"I've had a collect call from Tony," the doctor

reported. "He wants us to wire him one hundred dollars."

"What else does he say?" asked Jack.

"He wouldn't say. He was very brusque with me, just said he was getting along all right but was short of money. He gave me an address."

"Do you think he's in any trouble?"

"I don't know. At any rate, we ought to send him the money. You do that in the morning and I'll call this psychiatric social worker I know, and ask him to have a look in very diplomatically. He'll know how."

"Ask him to see if he can persuade Tony to come home," I put in from the extension.

"Even if he seems to be doing all right?"

"Doctor Johnson, he ought to be home with you."

"But you of all people ought to know," Dr. Johnson said quietly, "that Tony cannot be made to do anything he doesn't want to do."

"I know."

"Well, I'll keep in touch with you. Get a night's sleep, both of you."

We telegraphed the money in the morning and settled back to wait. By evening Western Union reported that the money had been delivered. There was no word from the doctor's friend. On the second day we asked Dr. Johnson for Jerry's telephone number so that we could call him ourselves. When we reached him we learned that he had found the house where Tony was staying, a rooming house in a shabby but respectable neighborhood. However, he had been unable to find Tony, but would try again the following day.

"I don't know how to thank you," Jack said, "for taking this time and trouble on behalf of strangers. It seems, in my situation, that I am always saying 'thank you' to people who are kinder than anyone has a right to expect."

"I've seen this sort of problem before," he replied. "I have some idea of what you're going through and I'd like to help. That's all."

On the third day Jerry called. He told us he had just put Tony on a plane and that he was even now flying back east.

Then he told us what had happened.

"I went back to the rooming house early in the afternoon," he said. "The landlady said, when I inquired, that Tony wasn't in. She seemed rather suspicious of me and disturbed about Tony. I told her I was a friend of his and she made some remarks about his never talking to anybody and never doing anything but sitting in the park all day. In fact, that was probably where I would find him now. The park was a dilapidated square down the street. I thanked her and left. Of course, I couldn't very well have asked for a description of my alleged friend, but it was not hard to guess who he was. There was only one young man sitting alone on a bench. His elbows were resting on his knees; he was just sitting there, staring at the ground.

"When I called him by name he looked up in terror. I don't know whether he thought perhaps I was a policeman. I told him quickly that I was a friend of Doctor Johnson's, that I had just happened to call him for some advice and he mentioned his friend Tony had just arrived in San

Diego. I told him I thought he might like to know somebody here.

" 'I'm perfectly capable of getting along by myself,' he told me. And I said I could see that.

" 'But it's always nice to know someone,' I said, 'when you are in a strange place. I'll probably be coming east myself one of these days and maybe you can return the favor.'

"This seemed to mollify him. From there I was able quite casually to suggest arranging his flight home. When Tony made no objection I understood he had been mortally afraid and was truly relieved to have been found.

"He came along after me like a child. We went back to the rooming house to pay his bill and get his things, which seemed to be only a pile of dirty clothes rumpled into a small overnight bag. Apparently he had been wearing the same clothes for two weeks. We had several hours before the plane was to leave and I thought I would take him to lunch. He did not speak all the way in the taxicab. We went into the airport lunchroom and sat in semidarkness far in back; because of Tony's dirty and unshaven appearance I wanted to spare him any embarrassment. I could not get him to say what he wanted to eat; instead, he waited for me to order and then said he'd have the same. Since I suspected he was very hungry, I ordered a meal much larger than I usually eat. Still he preserved his silence, so I took out a weekly newsmagazine and began to read. Then I saw that Tony was glancing at it and, noting the headline about the situation in the Far East, I ventured a remark about China. That interested him and he began a very serious, if not animated, conversation about the growing tensions between China and Russia and what they portended. He was amazingly well-informed and indeed knew a great deal more than I did about the land taken by the Russian empire from the Manchus. Your son is a real scholar.

"But then I'm telling you what you must already know. It's just that I found myself fascinated by the strange contrasts in your boy. I cannot get him out of my mind.

"When I asked him whether he wanted any dessert, he at first refused but something told me perhaps I had better ask again. When I mentioned pie à la mode Tony's face lighted.

" 'It's not on the menu,' he said.

" 'Ask the waitress for it, then,' I said.

" 'You ask her,' he whispered. I saw then how helpless he was. I realized he was afraid to speak to the waitress himself.

"Well," Jerry concluded, "I suppose you know this already but I'd just like to tell you that I've worked with Doctor Johnson, and if anyone can help your son I really believe he's the right man. He has marvelous sympathy and understanding, as I'm sure you've discovered by now. So I surely hope things turn out well for you."

"The one thing I've learned out of all this mess," Jack said when he had rung off, "is that there are some really wonderful people in the world. This man, and then Jim at The School and—" He turned away, but not before I could see that his eyes were shining with tears.

All of us in our separate places watched the hands of the clock crawl around the dial that wearying day. There was so much that could happen before we could rest, before Tony was back again. Jack called from the office. No, I hadn't heard yet. It was a long drive from the airport. Dr. Johnson would certainly wait until he reached home before calling. Unspoken in our minds was the thought that Tony might yet run away, that he might have left the plane at an intermediate stop.

Freddy and Sarah came home in the late afternoon. They had both taken their SAT's that day; I knew I should ask them how things had gone. And I did ask them, but I hardly heard what they said.

We were at the dinner table when Dr. Johnson's call came. Jack answered. The conversation was brief and when he came back to the table he met our questioning eyes by reporting simply.

"Tony's back, very tired. He's gone to sleep. Doctor Johnson will call us tomorrow after they have talked things over."

For the first time in almost three weeks we ourselves slept the night through.

The next day Dr. Johnson telephoned again and briefed us on the general events of the last few weeks:

Upon arriving out west Tony went to the YMCA, a wise enough choice. Unfortunately there was no vacancy, but the man at the desk advised him to take a furnished room temporarily. Then he went out to find a job—and found one, as a stock boy in a large drugstore. He worked there for three days and liked it well enough, but on the third day, he mistakenly put a stack of cartons in the wrong section and was reprimanded for it. That he would not tolerate, but being too timid to make any reply he simply walked out without collecting his pay for the three days' work.

For the next few days he did nothing except go swimming every afternoon at the Y where he had already paid for a membership. He also went in the evening with the intention of playing basketball, but at the doctor's prodding admitted he didn't play because the boys there were not friendly to him. This was in Tony's typical pattern, Doctor Johnson said, and I knew from long experience that very likely he had not even made any attempt to play but had just stood watching the game.

After another few days he decided he had better look for another job. In the want ads he saw an opening for messenger boy in a brokerage office. He went there, looked in at the door, and walked away because the place looked "too fancy." Probably, the doctor said, he realized he did not look neat enough to be acceptable there, although he would certainly never admit that. He then went to an employment agency, but while sitting in the waiting room he noticed two stenographers looking at him. He thought he heard them making some remarks about him so he simply got up and walked out of there, too.

"Do you think he imagined these people were talking about him?" I asked.

"Possibly," Dr. Johnson replied. "On the other

hand, they might very well have been saying something about him. By this time he had been away for nine or ten days without a change of clothing except one extra shirt. He must have looked pretty disreputable. I told him that, and he admitted he did not look very nice, but he believes that people ought not to judge you by your appearance.

"To make a long story short, he loafed away the rest of the time. He walked around looking in windows; one afternoon he went out to row on the lake. But mostly he just sat in the park near the rooming house, took his meals in a lunch wagon nearby. He admitted to me that he didn't speak to a living soul all the time he was away. There were some other fellows living in the rooming house, but he said he knows he does not know how to communicate with people, so he stayed away from them. Then, all of a sudden, he began to realize that his money was running short and he panicked. You know the rest."

That was the end of the short tale of Tony's venture into the outside world.

"What now?" I asked.

"We shall have to talk things over," Dr. Johnson said. "After I have had a chance to see Tony a few more times I will call you and we can arrange to meet."

We met two weeks later at a hotel near Dr. Johnson's home. Jack and I had invited the doctor to dinner. We were to spend the night at the hotel and drive back the next morning.

While we were waiting for Dr. Johnson in the lobby I thought of something. "What if he has decided he cannot keep Tony any more? What shall we do then?"

Jack did not answer. He just sat there, and for the first time in our life together I saw how he would look when he was old.

Dr. Johnson came striding in, his hand outstretched in greeting. He had a broad smile and I had a rush of gratitude on seeing him. Here was my son's security, a roof over his head, kindness, patience, all the qualities which the harsh world so sadly lacks.

We went in to dinner. "Well," Dr. Johnson began, "there are few misfortunes without some compensation. I know what you both went through while Tony was away. I know how you suffered and how he suffered, too. But I think also that he learned something."

Jack and I waited eagerly.

"I believe he learned that his omniscience is unreal and that he is not omnipotent. In short, I think he learned how sick he really is. He saw that he was unable to survive alone. Perhaps now he will be more willing to accept my direction and to make up his mind to stay."

"Have you discussed it?"

"Yes, and he has decided to go back to college and finish his education."

"I know you have no crystal ball," Jack said. "But have you, at this point, any thoughts at all about future possibilities beyond that?"

Dr. Johnson considered. "If Tony stays the way he is now, perhaps quieted down and more relaxed, I see him taking some sort of simple job that will not involve any relationship with people. That is, assuming he can maintain his equilibrium."

"And is he likely to maintain it?" Jack asked quietly.

He never has, I thought. We always go along for a few months and then there is a crisis.

"Well, you must understand he is very ill—"

As if we did not understand that!

"—and that almost any trauma of moderate severity might push him into even more severe withdrawal. Or on the other hand, it might push him in the other direction, into violent, uncontrolled behavior. In either case, he would have to be committed to a hospital."

"What do you mean by 'trauma'? What sort of blows?" I asked.

"Well, the death of either one of you, for instance. He will never be able to bear it."

"Since we are surely going to die," I said, "the prognosis for Tony is not very hopeful, is it?"

"One must always hope," the doctor replied. "Nothing is ever sure."

Once I had taken comfort from such platitudes. No more. We were simply marking time again, living from day to day, before the blow should come, whenever it might come. My mind went back to the time in the hospital when Dr. Brewster had told us, "If I were you I would just pray every morning when I got up for the strength to get through that one day."

I looked at Dr. Johnson. After all, I thought, you are doing the best you can with the meager knowledge you have at the present time. And what would we do without you? Without your shelter, where would Tony be? At least you put up with him. We are and must always be so grateful to you.

We shook hands, but later upstairs in our hotel room I lay long awake in the dark. I could not help thinking about too many of the psychiatrists to whom we have taken our insoluble problem.

They blur together in my mind. Bland men, bland as custard, the face behind the desk with a pad and flying pencil, a quiet manner and nothing to say. You have to admit that, if you want to be truthful with yourself; and lying awake night after night, going over the long years' experience, I have become coldly truthful.

How many times have Jack and I emerged from one of these conferences—after the cordial thanks and the sincere handshake and "Let's not lose hope, let's keep trying!"—and turned to each other and remarked, puzzled: "Such a nice man! What did he say?" And one or the other of us responds: "Come to think of it, what *did* he say?"

Jack never complains. For him there is no sense in questioning things that offer no present solution. But he grows visibly more tired and I know that his tiredness is emotional. His work does not tire him; it never did, he loves it. He still tells me how rewarding it is. But all he earns goes down the drain. The costs mount and Tony is the same.

We can put nothing aside. In spite of our above-average income we can save nothing toward old age or emergency. We still have two children to educate. Jane is almost finished but Sarah has four years of college and Freddy wants to be a doctor.

Sometimes I think that we ought to sell our

house. Prices have gone up. We could make a profit and move into a cheaper neighborhood. But then I think the profit would go to pay Dr. Johnson for only another year and a half. So basically, the move would solve nothing and we would have lost the home we love, where our children grew up and where the young trees that we planted are now giving shade. Then I think, yes, but at least we are not impoverished, not yet. As long as Jack is able to work we are able to meet the bills. What of all those families, and there are so many more of them, who cannot?

The other day I called for Jack at his office and we drove home in spangled light past dogwood white and starched as lace. It was spring-vacation time and the house was full. Jane's fiancé had come to dinner; they are to be married right after graduation in June. He was playing the violin, with Sarah at the piano. Gay measures of Mozart came floating through the open window, while Jane perched on the sill, a rapt audience of one. Freddy was at the hall telephone, lining up his social prospects for the weekend, no doubt, his biology textbooks littering the floor at his feet.

For a wordless moment we stopped to look at them. What wonderful young people they are! All the fruits of the earth are spread before them in bounty such as no other generation in history has seen. In spite of all that has been said and written about this generation, they are marvelous young people, most of them, eager and alert, reaching out so generously to the future and stretching back to take from the past the best of its heritage.

And we thought of Tony. Always, wherever we are, we think of Tony, who possibly more than any one of these others has so much sensitivity, so much perception, and who could have given so much to life.

It is three years since we have seen him. We are told that he has grown taller and broader; that his light hair is darkening. We have been promised a photograph and sometimes I want to see it and then again I do not want to see it at all. Often, when I am driving the car, I have the illusion his face is hovering before me, so clear, so well remembered. Then again, I am not even sure I would know him if I were to pass him on the street.

What will have happened when another three years have gone? Where will we be, and more importantly, where will *he* be?

Yet we live. We do our work and laugh and have some pleasures. Only at night when a thousand thoughts go running through my mind, the last is always for Tony, the last prayer for him and all the lonely who, like him, suffer and are afraid.

15

THIS, then, is the chronicle of our family up till now. This is as far as I can go. I ask myself why I have told the story at all, and the answer is: because from time to time in every life there comes a need to sort out long thoughts. I had to know where we stood and how this family of six human beings might have been changed by its experiences.

If in any small way our story can relieve other families, other parents, who have been carrying the same fearful burden, it will have been worth telling. I believe it can do so, even if it does no more than say: *You are not alone.* I know I gained strength when I learned my child was only one of thousands who had dropped silently out of sight. It gave me courage to see that so many others were enduring the same affliction with so much courage.

I don't think I had ever really known how brave people are, how patient, how trusting, until we began the rounds of hospitals and doctors' waiting rooms and I saw the long, unwinding tale of human pain. To Jack, of course, it was an old story: disfigurement, death, blasted hope. Gentle as he is, he had never become inured to it. But at least he had known that each of us is only a fragment in the endless pattern of life; that we are very, very small; that there are questions which we cannot answer and therefore must not torture ourselves by asking.

Why? I had cried a thousand times, demanding it of Jack, of myself and of the empty air. *Why our son? Why?*

Jack knew better than to ask. I had to learn.

But I have learned it at last. War and sickness, hatred and death exist in our world. We do our best to wipe them out, but our efforts are not perfect and we have to get along with what we have. We have to accept, if we are to go on living at all.

In our house we know that now. We understand that there are no automatic rewards for good behavior. You can be decent, industrious: Fate may rise against you all the same. You can be the most careful, thoughtful, loving father and mother—and your child may be like Tony.

We were talking about marriage one day, Sarah, Jane and I, while hemming linen towels for Jane's trousseau. The best plans notwithstanding, Jane said, marriage is always a giant step into the unknown.

Sarah spoke, a little uncertainly. "You and Dad surely could have had no idea of what would happen to you. Now and then I think of those times

with Tony when nobody at all knew what to do
next. You must have loved each other very much
to have come through it and still seem so happy
with each other."

"We did," I said. "And we do."

And I remembered something I had not thought
of in years: the woman who, at the time of peak
crisis, warned me to do something about Tony
before my husband sought out another woman.

I must have smiled because Jane asked what I
was thinking about.

They were old enough now to hear, so I told
them.

Sarah was shocked. Jane scoffed, "Oh, that
idiot!"

"I thought she was, too," I said. "And yet there
was a case ... It was when Tony was at The
School. There were several cases, in fact, but I
recall this one in particular because the boy was
something like Tony. His father couldn't stand
the situation; from what I heard, the parents
quarreled over it all the time, which was only
worse for the boy, of course. And finally the father
left and married someone else."

"How awful for the poor woman!" Jane cried.
"And for the boy. He probably thought it was his
fault."

"Strange," Sarah reflected, "that you can learn
something even from a tragedy like Tony's sickness. You find out what kind of a person you are,
what your values really are."

"I believe," Jane said slowly, "in a special way
we've all acquired a kind of toughness. You think,

well, one of the worst things imaginable has happened, so maybe we'll be able to manage anything else that comes along."

"I hope so," I said.

Toughness, yes, I thought; and along with it—really a part of it—a discerning compassion, too. You know that no matter what you've had, someone else is going through his own particular kind of hell. I truly believe that our daughters will bring to marriage a greater warmth of understanding, and that Freddy will be a wiser man and a wiser doctor because of the years with Tony.

More happily, Jack and I have become able to take tremendous joy in modest things. Because of our sick child we find more delight in the others who are well and in their simple affairs: a pie baked by Jane, a funny postcard from Freddy at the beach, Sarah's crashing mazurkas after dinner. Sometimes, on threatening, stormy nights, we have no words to express our thanks for those three, sleeping calmly under our roof. Every sense is alive with gratitude.

One day this summer I found my old easel at the back of the attic. I had not touched it in more than twelve years, since the time Tony had first gone to Dr. Maxwell.

Why do you paint? Do you feel a real need for it?

The canvas that had been on the easel the day I thrust it away was on it still, an empty rectangle except for one arc of wet-looking green paint. What had I intended to draw? The plume of a wave? A branch, or an arm in a green sleeve?

Suddenly I was excited, I wanted to experience again the delicious flow and curve of color. I took the easel downstairs and planted it on the porch. I stood before it. I had no idea of what I wanted to do.

The line of green curved downward to the lower left. I stretched it up to the right and it became a line of rough dune grass, bending in the Nantucket wind. I drew a figure lying in the grass with legs crossed. The sunlight quivered. The salt air blew. It was so easy; it painted itself.

Hanna came in. I heard her standing there and saw the curiosity on her face. But she did not speak and in a moment went away again.

I painted all afternoon. When dinnertime came and everyone was home, I wiped my hands and put the brushes away. I was not finished with it but the picture was recognizable: a boy lying with one arm flung out and a blade of long grass in his mouth.

"That's good!" Jack said. "That's very good!"

"You've drawn Tony," Freddy said.

"No, no, it's just any boy."

"But he looks like Tony."

I didn't think so. Surely I hadn't intended that. But perhaps the line of the straight nose . . . ? The face was really only sketched in; yet if Freddy wanted to see Tony there, it was all right.

"You can still do it," Jack said wonderingly. And then: "Why did you?"

We speak to one another, after all these years, in a kind of shorthand. So I knew he was asking me anxiously whether this was to be therapy for me, to dispel some new anxieties.

"All at once I love it again and want to," I answered. "That's the only valid reason for me."

Jack smiled.

"I would like to have it for my room when it's finished," Freddy said.

"Of course. I'm so glad you want it!"

I'm sure he thought I was pleased because he admired my work. But that was not it at all. I was thinking: *It looks like your brother and still you want to keep it where you'll see it every day.* That meant Freddy's thoughts of his brother were good ones, wholesome thoughts. And I was glad. He had accepted Tony, the way Tony is.

No more mirages then, for us. No more false fancies that this or that analyst is going to talk Tony's sickness out of him or "work it through." This family knows what it has. The sickness is there, that's all. And it's going to be there until somebody in science finds out what it is and how to get rid of it. That may be ten years from now or tomorrow. But someone will find out. From all that we keep hearing, it will be sooner rather than later.

So we don't give up. We accept, but we keep a certain rational hope, a small fire glowing. We know that we have done our best. Often we feel that our best should have been better. But it was our best and that, after all, is the most anyone can do. And keep on doing.

Yet there is one thing more. *Tony knows that we are doing our best for him.* He knows that we will never give up, that we will never allow him, figuratively speaking, to die. We have managed to keep him in touch with the world of the living; we have made him live, too, and learn as much as he can. We have refused to shut him away. It is still true that he cannot talk to us; there is too much anguish for him to talk to us or to see us. But he understands that we are on his side. This only came to my mind a short while ago, and it was a revelation.

I think of him that day in the hospital and the way he described home: "Birds coming to the feeder, the print of the covered wagons over my desk."

I hear again his anxious voice on the telephone calling from The School. It was after one of our visits, when he had been especially abusive.

"I don't understand why I act that way!" he cried. "I never WANT to. I really know you're so good, you're trying to help me. I really know it. Try to remember that about me, no matter what I do. . . . I wish I could be better to you."

Now and then he wants something, a set of skis or some lessons in the classical guitar. Sometimes Dr. Johnson hesitates.

"We shall have to ask your parents. I can't authorize you to spend that much without asking them first."

"They'll say yes," Tony assures him. "You know they will." Dr. Johnson reports Tony is a little annoyed to think that anyone might have a doubt. "You know they will do anything for me! *They love me!*"

And then I am sure that everything we have done, everything we have spent, suffered, tried and so often wasted, has been worth it. If we had to, we would do it all over again. Just possibly that giant effort of ours has been some part of such strength as Tony has.

Under all the fear and anger, he has faith in our love. When his mind is clear, and perhaps even in clouded hours, he knows our love will last. It will be there always; it is there now, waiting for the joyous day when Tony may come home to us all again.

Have You Read These Current Bestsellers from SIGNET?

☐ **THE FRENCH LIEUTENANT'S WOMAN by John Fowles.**
By the author of **The Collector** and **The Magus**, a haunting love story of the Victorian era. Over one year on the N.Y. Times Bestseller List and an international bestseller. "Filled with enchanting mysteries, charged with erotic possibilities ．．．"—Christopher Lehmann-Haupt, **N.Y. Times** (#W4479—$1.50)

☐ **LOVE STORY by Erich Segal.** The story of love fought for, love won, and love lost. It is America's Romeo and Juliet. And it is one of the most touching, poignant stories ever written. A major motion picture starring Ali MacGraw and Ryan O'Neal. (#Q4414—95¢)

☐ **JENNIE, The Life of Lady Randolph Churchill by Ralph G. Martin.** In JENNIE, Ralph G. Martin creates a vivid picture of an exciting woman, Lady Randolph Churchill, who was the mother of perhaps the greatest statesman of this century, Winston Churchill, and in her own right, one of the most colorful and fascinating women of the Victorian era. (#W4213—$1.50)

☐ **THE AFFAIR by Morton Hunt.** Explores one of the mos engrossing and profoundly troubling of contemporary concerns. Morton Hunt allows the reader to enter this secret underground world through the actual words and experiences of eight unfaithful men and women. (#Y4548—$1.25)

THE NEW AMERICAN LIBRARY, INC.,
P.O. Box 999, Bergenfield, New Jersey 07621

Please send me the SIGNET BOOKS I have checked above. I am enclosing $_____(check or money order—no currency or C.O.D.'s). Please include the list price plus 15¢ a copy to cover mailing costs.

Name_____

Address_____

City_____State_____Zip Code_____
Allow at least 3 weeks for delivery